D0715911

THE STORY OF READING

View of Reading from Caversham by J. Farington, 1794

THE STORY OF READING

including Caversham, Tilehurst, Calcot, Earley and Woodley

DAPHNE PHILLIPS

COUNTRYSIDE BOOKS

NEWBURY BERKSHIRE

FIRST PUBLISHED 1980
Reprinted 1981, 1983, 1986
© Daphne Phillips 1980

COUNTRYSIDE BOOKS
3 Catherine Road
Newbury Berkshire

ISBN 0 905392 07 8

The cover illustration is a view of Reading
from Kennet Mouth by Fletcher, 1840, showing the river Kennet
and the newly opened G.W.R. line

Designed by Mon Mohan

Printed in England by
J. W. Arrowsmith Ltd., Bristol

Contents

Reading and its adjacent countryside, by Thomas Pride, 1790.

Acknowledgements

The Story of Reading has been based mainly upon sources available in the Berkshire Local History Collection at Reading Library, and I am grateful to Mr M. E. Asser, the County Librarian, for the use of the material and for the loan of many of the prints, maps and photographs reproduced in the book.

Mr Leslie North very kindly loaned the photographs of St Anne's Well and John Blagrave's monument. Mr H. H. Dennis took those of the Hexagon and the Railway Station especially for the book. Mr Robert Lacey loaned the photograph of Mr and Mrs F. G. Miles at Reading Aerodrome, Metal Box Ltd the photograph of Queen's House, and Sutton's Seeds Ltd the aerial view of the Royal Seed Establishment. Miss Susan Read of Reading Museum supplied the photograph of School Road, Tilehurst. The conjectural views of Reading Abbey were drawn by the late R. W. Ford of Earley.

To all the above, and to the publishers, Nicholas and Suzanne Battle, for their constant help and encouragement, I would like to record my thanks.

DAPHNE PHILLIPS

The Site

The rivers Thames and Kennet have played a vital part in the making of Reading. In the beginning their waters helped to shape the gravel terraces on which the original settlement was established, and the tendency of both rivers to overflow their banks has continued to influence the direction of the town's development. Modern Reading extends over thousands of acres of firm ground which once belonged to Tilehurst, Burghfield, Shinfield, Earley and Caversham, but it is still cleft by the valley of the Thames and deeply indented from the southwest by the flood plain of the Kennet. Industrial estates are now filling the once marshy gap between the town and the south bank of the Thames, and spreading out to the west of Basingstoke Road, but there are still green fields beside the Kennet, and at Coley, barely a mile from the town centre, cattle graze as they have done for centuries in the low-lying meadows beside the Holy Brook.

Early settlers were attracted to the site by the ford across the Kennet. Here the river, making its way between the gravel terraces, broke into a number of shallow streams. On either side the terraces extended for two miles to east and west, providing a dry approach to the ford and firm ground on which a settlement could be established above the level of normal flooding.

The site had many other advantages. To the south and west the hillsides were suitable for growing corn. To the east there were forests providing timber for building, food for swine and wild beasts for hunting. As well as an abundant supply of fresh water the rivers provided fish, reeds for thatching, and lush meadows for pasturing cattle.

To the north was the river Thames. This was separated from the terraces by a low-lying area which was usually swampy and often flooded, but the site was so close to Kennet-mouth that the Thames was quickly reached by water. The nearness of the great waterway, which from early times carried barges between London and Reading and Oxford, enabled Reading to develop into a thriving inland port.

The site was not only easily accessible by water but by land routes. Probably in Saxon times two major routes meeting here promoted the growth of Reading as a trading centre. One of these routes ran from east to west, between London and Bristol; the other from north to south, between the midlands, Oxford, Winchester and Southampton. The routes met at the Kennet ford.

The north-south route crossed the Thames also at Caversham. A bridge existed here by 1231 (the date of the earliest surviving record) and may have existed for some years before that. Responsibility for the bridge was shared, in the middle ages, between the abbot of Reading and the lord of the manor of Caversham, both of whom levied tolls for the upkeep of the bridge. People who were too poor to pay the tolls crossed by the ferry. A document also issued in 1231 commanded the keeper of Windsor Forest to deliver one good oak to the sergeant of Caversham, to make a boat for ferrying poor people across the river.

In course of time the ford across the Kennet streams was replaced by Seven Bridges, a name which clung to the street now called Bridge Street long after most of the streams had been culverted and the bridges reduced in number. On the north side of Seven Bridges lay the most ancient part of the town, and it is believed that the earliest church in Reading was built on the site of St Mary's. St Mary's Butts was previously known as Old Street, a sign that it was already old in medieval times.

Another bridge across the Kennet was built further downstream at High Bridge. This carried a road directly to the abbey and into the eastern side of the town which grew up after the abbey was founded in 1121. The market was transferred from its original site in Old Street to a new market place outside the abbey gate. The eastern side of the town was to remain for centuries the business and administrative heart of Reading.

The waters of the Kennet served the town in many ways. Long before the Norman Conquest they were driving mills to grind the corn. When Reading Abbey was built the northernmost arm of the Kennet, which became known as the Holy Brook, was diverted so that it could drive the abbey mill and serve the washing and drainage needs of the monks; (their drinking water was piped from a spring on Whitley Hill). Later, the availability of the Kennet's fast running streams to operate fulling mills was a key factor in the development of cloth making as the town's leading industry.

In the reign of Henry VIII the members of the merchant guild, whose hall was situated close to the Kennet near High Bridge, complained that their meetings were constantly interrupted by the deafening racket made by washerwomen working on the river bank and using wooden battledores to beat the dirt out of the clothes. In the reign of Elizabeth I an attempt was made to keep the water of the Holy Brook clean, for purposes of brewing, baking and dressing meat, by an order forbidding people to use the brook for the drainage of hogsties, stables or gutters, or for watering horses, or for the disposal of household garbage.

Wharves were built along the Kennet in early medieval times; the town wharf on the north bank near High Bridge being conveniently placed for the market. More wharves were built as commercial traffic on the rivers increased. In the 18th century the Kennet navigation between Newbury and Reading was opened, and the early 19th century saw the completion of the long-awaited Kennet and Avon Canal, linking Bristol and London by water. The Kennet wharves must then have been the scene of constant activity.

Thirty years after the Kennet and Avon Canal began to be used it was superseded by the Great Western Railway. Once again Reading, situated on the main line between London and Bristol, reaped enormous benefits. Reading's accessibility by water, road, railway, and 20th century motorway has brought it almost continuous prosperity, and enabled it to develop into the important centre of commerce, communications, industry and administration which it is today.

The Early Settlers

Stone implements shaped by men of the Palaeolithic and Neolithic Ages; bronze axeheads, swords and spearheads; signs of a Bronze Age barrow at Whitley, and of an Iron Age dwelling at Southcote; pottery, weapons and brooches of many ages dredged up from the Thames, all show that people had begun to live in, or pass through, the Reading area thousands of years ago. Roman coins, pottery, horseshoes and other relics have survived in plenty from the centuries when Britain was part of the Roman empire, and a Romano-British cemetery has been found near Kennet-mouth.

None of the evidence suggests an early settlement of any size or significance. Barely ten miles to the south-west was Calleva, the chief town of the British tribe of the Atrebates, who occupied an area which now includes Berkshire and parts of Hampshire, Wiltshire and Surrey. During the Roman occupation Calleva became the Romano-British town of Silchester and continued to be the centre for trade, administration and culture in this part of the country. Although the site of Reading must have been well known to the Romans no trace of a Roman building, military or domestic, has been found in the town, and no Roman road passed this way.

Silchester, however, was destined to decay after the withdrawal of the Romans from Britain early in the 5th century. The waves of invaders who next came from across the sea were fierce, Teutonic tribes, who came to dispossess the native Britons by fire and sword. A century or more of bloodshed and chaos ensued in which the old organised way of life came to an end, and civilised towns which had flourished under Roman rule were left uninhabited and neglected. Although the history of Britain during that dark time is obscure, the evidence of archaeology and place names suggests that Saxon tribes had begun to establish settlements in the middle Thames valley by the beginning of the 6th century. Probably about that time the people of a man named Reada came to settle on the land near Kennet-mouth.

These people were called the Readingas, and so Reading got its name.

There are no records of the lives or fortunes of the inhabitants of Reading during the next three to four hundred years, but by the 9th century, when the town first appears in the history books, many changes had taken place and a new way of life had been established.

After the native British tribes had been overcome or driven into remote strongholds, the old tribal regions were redivided among the conquerors, and eventually England was reorganised into seven kingdoms. Of these, the south-western kingdom of Wessex and the midland kingdom of Mercia were two of the most powerful. For a long time the area which later became Berkshire was in dispute between these two, but by the middle of the 9th century it had finally become part of Wessex. By that time, too, the shires had been formed as units for local administration and defence. Reading itself had achieved some distinction as a royal *vill,* a place where the king had an estate which helped to support him and his household, and which served as an administrative centre. In Saxon Berkshire, Reading was smaller and less important than Wallingford. The latter was a fortified borough and one of those which, during the 10th century, were permanently garrisoned for the defence of Wessex against the Danes.

In the 7th century Christianity was brought back to the Thames Valley by Birinus, the first apostle of Wessex and its first bishop. In 635 he baptised Cynegils, King of the West Saxons, at Dorchester-on-Thames, and was given Dorchester as the seat of his bishopric. Nearly twenty years later Christianity was reintroduced into the midlands by Peada, King of the Middle Angles, making both kingdoms which laid claim to Berkshire Christian. Conversion of kings, however, did not necessarily mean that all their people accepted the new religion. Many remained stubbornly heathen, and a generation or more was to pass before worship of the old pagan gods, Tiw, Thunor, Woden and Frig, was abandoned in favour of Christian worship.

Nothing is known of a church in Reading during that early period. A nunnery is believed to have existed here in the 10th century. Traditionally it was founded by Queen Aelfthryth to expiate the murder of her stepson, King Edward, at Corfe in 978, but no trace of the building has ever been discovered. It may well have been totally destroyed in the Danish raid of 1006.

The trouble with the Danes began in 835 when the first boatloads of heathen marauders raided Sheppey. In the years that followed, other and more terrible raids were carried out on the eastern and southern coasts of Britain. Towns and villages were plundered and burned; the inhabitants brutally slaughtered. The English, by that time a settled and peace-loving people, seemed powerless to oppose them, and by the middle of the 9th century the Danes had gained sufficient footholds to be able to winter in England.

In 865 a major invasion took place. A large and powerful Danish army landed in East Anglia and ravaged the countryside for several months before the local people succeeded in buying peace with a heavy tribute. In 866 the army invaded the kingdom of Northumbria and occupied York. In 867-8 they took up winter quarters in the Mercian town of Nottingham. By this time the forces of Mercia and Wessex had combined to confront them; peace terms were agreed, and the Danes retired to Northumbria. But not for long. In the winter of 869-70 they came south again to East Anglia. There they overthrew the army of the young King Edmund, bound the king to a tree and shot at him until his body was full of arrows, plundered the monasteries and committed many other atrocities.

The Anglo-Saxon Chronicle, the history of England which was begun in the 9th century and records these terrible events, contains the earliest known reference to Reading when it reaches the year 871. "In this year", it says, "the army came into Wessex to Reading."

It does not mention the inhabitants; they had, perhaps, wisely fled before the enemy arrived. The Danes dug themselves in at Reading, building a rampart on the western side, which was not defended by the rivers. Three days after their arrival a party of them, led by two Danish earls, rode out towards Englefield. There a West Saxon force, under the leadership of Ealdorman Aethelwulf, was waiting for them. A battle took place in which many Danes were killed, including one of their earls, and the rest were driven back to Reading.

Four days afterwards Aethewulf was joined by the main army of the West Saxons led by King Ethelred and his brother Alfred. The entire Saxon force marched on Reading determined to regain possession of it, and rid Wessex of the Danes. The Saxon assault was directed mainly upon the gateway through the rampart, and at that point fierce and bloody fighting took place. Many Danes and Saxons were killed; among them Ealdorman Aethewulf. The attack failed. The Saxons were forced to retreat, leaving the way open for the Danes to advance into Wessex.

Ethelred and Alfred re-formed their army on the slopes of the Berkshire Downs where, a few days after the fight at Reading, they won a famous victory over the Danes at the Battle of Ashdown. The cost to both sides was heavy. Thousands of men lay dead and dying on the battlefield. For the Danes, the loss of several of their leaders, including a king and five earls, was fatal, and by nightfall they were fleeing back to their camp at Reading.

Unfortunately, the Saxons' triumph at Ashdown could have no lasting effect upon so strong and numerous an enemy. A fortnight later the two sides met again near Basing, and on this occasion victory went to the Danes. In April 871 King Ethelred died and was succeeded by Alfred, whose 28-year reign was largely taken up with the continuing struggle against the Danes.

The summer of 871 saw the arrival of Danish reinforcements at Reading, where they remained for several months before moving to winter quarters in London. For more than a century after that, nothing is known of events in Reading. Yet, when next the town is mentioned in the *Chronicle,* time seems almost to have stood still.

"1006 . . After midsummer the Danish fleet came to Sandwich, and did just as they were accustomed, ravaged, burned and slew as they went. Then the king ordered the whole nation from Wessex to Mercia to be called out, and they were out on military service against the Danish army the whole autumn, yet it availed no whit more than it had done before . . . and the Danish army then came after Martinmas to its sanctuary, the Isle of Wight, and procured for themselves everywhere whatever they needed; and then towards Christmas they betook themselves to the entertainment waiting them, out through Hampshire into Berkshire to Reading; and always they observed their ancient custom, lighting their beacons as they went."

After Reading, the Danes set fire to Wallingford and burned it down. Next they went by way of Cholsey up onto the Downs, where they marched in triumph past the site of their former defeat at Ashdown. Then they turned southwards across the Kennet and made their way back to the sea, laden with plunder.

In 1017 Cnut the Dane became king of all England. During his reign many Danes were granted possessions in England, and Reading passed for a while to a Dane named Tovi the Proud. But an Englishman named Godwine was made Earl of Wessex and became one of the most powerful men in the land.

The Norman Landlords

When the childless King Edward the Confessor died in January 1066 Harold, son of Earl Godwine, was chosen king of England and crowned at Westminster. Nine months later, after defeating the army of the rival Norwegian claimant to the throne at Stamford Bridge in Yorkshire, Harold marched to the Sussex coast to repel another claimant, William, Duke of Normandy, and met his death at Hastings.

During the battle Harold's standard was set up near the summit of a hill, and here, on the spot where he fell, was later sited the high altar of Battle Abbey. This abbey was founded by William I in thanksgiving for his victory, and, among other endowments, he gave it an estate at Reading known as Battle Manor. This link was the origin of the names of Battle Farm, Battle Hospital, Battle Ward and Battle School, all situated on land which was once part of Battle Manor.

Although many leading Englishmen were at first prepared to accept William as king, and some were allowed to hold office under him, the severity of Norman rule soon led to uprisings in many parts of England. When these had been suppressed, Normans replaced Englishmen in positions of power and, all over the country, English lands were given to William's trusted followers. With Norman landlords controlling every town, village and hamlet, the plight of the English became far more wretched, since most of them were tied to the land on which they lived and bound by harsh laws to serve their Norman lords.

This reversal in the fortunes of the English is clearly seen in the survey which William caused to be carried out some twenty years after he came to throne. His purpose was to make a record of the extent of the lands and properties held by himself and by his subjects, and the value of the revenues and services which could be expected from them. In 1086 his commissioners visited each county and took evidence on oath from the sheriff, the barons, the Frenchmen who had settled in the area, the priests, reeves, and other men representing each village.

Everywhere the same questions were asked. What manorial estates existed? Who held them, and who had done so previously in the time of Edward the Confessor? What was their value now, and what had it been then? What other holdings were there, and how much rent did they yield? How many peasants of various degrees worked on the land, and how many ploughteams were available? What was the extent, number and value of other local resources, such as arable lands, pastures, woodlands, mills and fisheries? And so on. The king's demands were bitterly resented by the English; one chronicler complained that "there was not one single hide, nor one yard of land, nor even — it is shame to tell, though it seemed to him no shame to do — an ox, nor a cow, nor a swine, was left that was not set down in his writ."

Before the end of the year the survey was completed and the information delivered to the king at Winchester. Some time later the numerous parchment rolls compiled so painstakingly by the commissioners were copied out into two large volumes which, since the 12th century, have been known as Domesday Book.

Reading, Domesday Book recorded, belonged to the king, and had formerly belonged to King Edward. It included a small borough and two manors, or agricultural estates. In the borough the king owned 28 plots yielding £5 a year in rents. Unfortunately the commissioners were not interested in how many houses stood on these plots, or how many people lived in them. Neither did they record any kind of trade or other activity in the borough.

One large plot and three acres of meadow belonged to the Norman Henry de Ferrers, an ancestor of the Earls of Derby and already one of the largest landowners in England, having estates in fifteen counties. In Berkshire he had received estates formerly held by the English sheriff, Godric, who had been killed at Hastings. As the king's representative in the county Godric had maintained this property in Reading for the purpose of entertaining important or official visitors, a responsibility which now rested with Henry de Ferrers.

Of the two agricultural estates, one belonged to the king and one to Battle Abbey. The king's estate had land sufficient to be worked by 40 ploughteams, although 56 ploughteams were counted, plus 85 peasants. On the Kennet four mills were working, and these were worth 35 shillings in rent. There were also three fisheries, worth 14 shillings and 6 pence, pasture worth 16 shillings and 6 pence, 150 acres of meadow, and woodland providing food for swine, for which payment

Old St Giles' Mill, in Mill Lane, shortly before it was demolished in 1900 to make way for the tramways depot. One of the corn mills counted in the Domesday survey may have stood upon this site.

of 100 swine was made. The estate had increased in value, having been worth £40 in the time of King Edward and being now worth £48.

The estate belonging to Battle Abbey included the only church known to have existed in Reading at that time. Although Domesday Book gives the church no name, merely recording that it had been formerly held by the abbess Leveva and was now worth £3 a year to the abbot of Battle, it was almost certainly an early church on the site of St Mary's, which stands in the most ancient part of the town. Along with the church the Abbot owned 29 dwellings in Reading, from which he received 28 shillings and 8 pence rent, 12 acres of meadow, woodland yielding five swine, land for seven ploughteams, two mills and two fisheries.

Round about Reading other estates were recorded whose history has since become closely linked with that of the borough. At Southcote the Norman Walter de Braose held an estate which had formerly belonged to an Englishman named Brictward. It included land for three ploughteams, a mill worth 18 shillings and a fishery worth 50 pence. Further upstream, Brictward had owned a smaller estate at Calcot, which was now in the hands of the Count of Evreux. At Caversham extensive lands and a mill were held by a powerful Norman, Walter Giffard, while at Earley an estate was held by Osbern Giffard.

Domesday Book shows that the great majority of the population at that time was engaged in agriculture, or in associated activities such as flour milling. The peasant's life must have been an unrelenting struggle to produce enough food for his lord and his lord's household, as well as for himself and his family, and to pay whatever other dues were demanded of him. The emphasis on the extent of arable lands and the number of ploughteams leaves a picture in the mind of a bare, wintry landscape, dotted with ploughmen plodding interminably behind their scrawny oxen. There must have been times of haymaking and harvest, and even seasonal merrymakings, but the commissioners were not concerned with these. The Domesday picture of the hardship of the peasants' lives was confirmed by English chroniclers of the time. One of these wrote: "The king and the head men loved much, and overmuch, covetousness in gold and silver, and recked not how sinfully it might be got, provided it came to them. The king gave his land as dearly for rent as he possibly could . . ."

To make matters worse, the Domesday survey was followed by "a very heavy and toilsome and sorrowful year in England, through murrain of cattle; and corn and fruits were at a stand; and so great unpropitiousness in weather as no one can easily think; so great was the thunder and lightning that it killed many men; and ever it grew worse with men, more and more."

In Domesday Book Reading and Wallingford are the only places in Berkshire described as boroughs. It is not known when Reading achieved this status, which may have been granted because of the town's growing importance as a trading centre, but the existence of coins minted in Reading in the reign of Edward the Confessor shows that it had been a borough at least since his time. Boroughs were privileged to hold regular markets. They also served as centres for royal administration from which the king's agents collected dues owing to him from the shire. Wallingford was still by far the more important borough. Domesday Book presents it as a flourishing market town, several times larger than Reading, and numbering a fair proportion of Frenchmen among its inhabitants. Its strategic importance had been confirmed by the Normans; the old Saxon earthworks had been superseded by an imposing castle guarding the river crossing.

At Windsor, too, the king was building a castle for himself; while at Abingdon, although no town yet existed, there was an already venerable abbey, founded in Saxon times. Domesday Reading lacked any such distinguishing feature, but it was not to do so much longer.

The Abbey

The abbey whose power and magnificence were to dominate Reading for four centuries, and whose pathetic ruins now stand beside the Kennet, was founded by Henry I in 1121 and dissolved by Henry VIII in 1539. Its founder was not very much more religious than its dissolver. Henry I was an efficient statesman and administrator, whose reign brought peace and order to the country, but he ruled with an iron hand and was notoriously cruel, licentious and avaricious. Historical evidence suggests that he had connived at the murder of his brother, William Rufus, in order to gain the throne for himself. In November 1120, when he had reigned for twenty years, Henry's only legitimate son was drowned when the White Ship sank off the coast of France. Grief at his loss is believed to have moved Henry to found a religious house, and to this cause he proved generous.

The site he chose was his own borough of Reading, a place of growing importance not only as a market town but as a stopping place for travellers to and from London, Southampton, the west country and the midlands. It was also situated in countryside which was beautiful as well as fertile. The area marked out for the abbey and its precincts occupied about 30 acres of gently rising ground, bounded on the south side by the Kennet and overlooking the valley of the Thames to the north. On the western side the abbey closely adjoined the town, and its busiest gateway opened onto a street which was soon to become the site of the weekly market.

The first eight monks came from the abbey of Cluny in Burgundy, where the Cluniac order had been founded as a reformed branch of the Benedictine, or Black Monk, order. They were joined by several others from the Cluniac priory at Lewes, Sussex, and on 18 June 1121 a religious community was established in Reading under the rule of a prior. The first abbot, Hugh I, was appointed in 1123.

Henry's initial endowment of the abbey included the manors and churches of Reading, Leominster in Herefordshire, and Cholsey,

Reading Abbey, a conjectural view from the south-east across the Kennet, showing Orts Bridge, the monks' dormitory (with the tower of St Laurence's behind it), the chapter house and the abbey church.

Reading Abbey, a conjectural view from the north-west across the Forbury, showing the abbey church and the abbot's house to the left of the inner gateway.

together with their woods, fields, pastures, meadows and rivers, mills and fisheries, chapels, cemeteries, oblations and tithes; and also the manor of Thatcham and the church of Wargrave. This endowment was followed by many other substantial gifts from the king, his family and his successors on the throne, so that by the 14th century Reading Abbey had become one of the ten wealthiest Benedictine monasteries in England. The most significant of Henry's gifts, so far as the subsequent history of the town of Reading was concerned, were those of his own estate at Reading, and of the church and estate formerly belonging to Battle Abbey, which he had recovered by exchanging it for a manor in Sussex. Through these gifts the abbots of Reading became lords of both manors, and so gained control over the town's affairs as well as over the three parish churches of St Mary, St Laurence and St Giles.

In his foundation charter Henry granted specific rights and privileges to the abbey. Its monks and their servants were to be exempt from tolls and other customary payments exacted from persons travelling "by land and by water, in passage of bridges, and in the seaports, throughout England." The abbot and his monks were to hold the local court of justice and have "entire jurisdiction in cases of assault, thefts and murders, shedding of blood and breaches of the peace, in the same manner as belongs to the royal authority, and of all transgressions. But if the abbot and monks shall at any time fail to do justice, the king may compel them, provided that he does not diminish the privileges of the Church of Reading." The king also ordained that, on the death of an abbot of Reading, all the possessions of the monastery, together with all rights and customs, should remain at the disposal of the prior, monks and chapter of Reading. The charter made it clear that the abbot had no rents for his own use, but enjoyed them in common with his brethren, and that he must not bestow the alms of the abbey on his kindred or on other persons, but must use them for the entertainment of the poor, of pilgrims, or of guests.

As an entertainer of the poor, of pilgrims, and of guests Reading Abbey soon became famous. Only a few years after its foundation the chronicler, William of Malmesbury, wrote that Henry I had built it "in a spot calculated for the reception of almost all who might have occasion to travel to the more populous cities of England, where he placed monks of the Cluniac Order, who are at this day a noble pattern of holiness, and an example of unwearied and delightful hospitality." Guests, he added, might be seen arriving every hour, and they consumed more than the inmates.

The poor and the sick alike benefited from the charity and care of the monks. As early as 1134 a leper house was built there, which served as a refuge for the outcast sufferers from this disease. A number of poor people were permanently supported out of the alms of the abbey, and every day the orts, or food scraps, were distributed to the poor at Orts Bridge (now known as Blake's Bridge) just outside the abbey's eastern gate. A hospitium, or guest house, had existed at the abbey almost from the beginning, but before the end of the 12th century the numbers of visitors had grown so great that it had to be replaced by a larger building. The hospitium of St John the Baptist, whose remains may still be seen on the north side of St Laurence's churchyard, was some distance away from the strictly monastic buildings and conveniently close to the town for the reception of travellers. Here a few day's food and accommodation were provided for the needy as well as for the wealthier people who were expected to contribute to the abbey's expenses.

The abbey took many years to build, and progress on its noble and beautifully decorated church was slow, but long before it was completed pilgrims began to flock to Reading. They came not only to wonder at and worship in a fine new church, but to pray at the shrine in which was preserved the abbey's most precious relic, the hand of St James the Apostle. This was another of the royal founder's gifts, and one which assured the abbey's fame. Appropriately, the coat of arms borne by the abbey consisted of three golden scallop shells on a blue ground. The scallop shell was one of the symbols of St James, often represented as a pilgrim, and it became a symbol widely associated with pilgrims.

Those who made the journey to Reading could also cross the Thames to visit another famous place of pilgrimage, the shrine of Our Lady of Caversham. This was in a chapel dedicated to St Mary, all traces of which have long been destroyed, but it is believed to have been founded in the 12th century and to have stood near St Peter's Church. The shrine contained a silver-plated statue of Our Lady standing beneath a silver canopy, and was believed at one time to have miraculous powers. It had been enriched by gifts from many patrons, including royalty and successive Earls of Pembroke, who were lords of the manor of Caversham. In 1439 Isabel, Countess of Warwick, bequeathed to it a crown of gold and jewels with which the crown was to be encrusted. Lamps and candles burned day and night around the shrine.

On Caversham Bridge, near the northern end, stood another chapel,

The holy well of St Anne, whose healing waters brought many pilgrims to Caversham in the middle ages.

built in the 13th century and dedicated to St Anne, Mother of Our Lady. This too was a place of pilgrimage, although it also served as a tollhouse to collect payments for the upkeep of the bridge on behalf of the lord of the manor. A chapel dedicated to the Holy Ghost at the Reading end of the bridge served a similar purpose on behalf of the

Abbot of Reading. In Caversham, not far from the bridge, St Anne's Well was believed to have healing properties.

At Reading Abbey the guests often included the highest and mightiest in the land. In the middle ages, before there was a permanent seat of government, the king moved ceaselessly from place to place in England or in his dominions in France. With him travelled his court, his government officials, his treasure and his household staff. He needed the kind of large and generous accommodation which could only be provided at a wealthy castle or abbey. Reading Abbey became a favourite stopping place for kings, and during the 400 years of its monastic life it was the scene of many grand and ceremonious events.

The first of these was the burial of its founder in January 1136. Henry I had died in December 1135, whilst on a visit to Normandy. His body, embalmed and sewn into a bull's hide, was brought back to England and buried with great pomp before the high altar of Reading Abbey church. His nephew and successor, King Stephen, together with the Archbishop of Canterbury and many other priests and noblemen, were present. In the following December, on the anniversary of Henry's death, his widowed queen, Adeliza, visited the church and, at an impressive ceremony, laid a richly embroidered pall on the altar. At the same time she endowed the abbey with lands for the salvation of the dead king's soul, and to provide for a fitting annual memorial of his death.

In 1163 King Henry II stayed at the abbey to witness a trial by combat between Henry de Essex and Robert de Montfort. Essex had been accused by Montfort of cowardice and treachery during a battle which had taken place in Wales some years before. Essex had denied the charge and a judicial trial by combat had been arranged. The duel took place on an island in the Thames which was later named, after the victor, De Montfort Island.

Essex was so severely wounded that he was believed dead, and his body was taken back to the abbey for burial. But he was not dead. Under the care of the monks he lived to tell the strange story of how he had been defeated. In the midst of the fight, he said, a vision had appeared to him of the martyred King Edmund dressed in shining armour, and beside him the vision of another dead knight, Gilbert de Cereville, whose cruel death in prison had been brought about by Essex himself. Overcome with remorse and dazzled by the light of the vision, Essex had fought wildly and had received the almost fatal wound. His defeat having proved his guilt, he was outlawed and deprived of his estates, but allowed to spend the rest of his life in

The trial by combat between Henry de Essex and Robert de Montfort, 8 April 1163.

seclusion at Reading Abbey.

By 1164 the work of building and embellishing the abbey church was nearing completion. On April 19 it was solemnly dedicated by the Archbishop of Canterbury, Thomas Becket, in the presence of Henry II and an impressive gathering of priests and dignitaries. A few months later Becket and Henry were to part in anger, and six years later the Archbishop was murdered at Canterbury.

In 1185 King Henry II received at Reading Abbey Heraclius, Patriarch of Jerusalem, and Roger, Master of the Knights Hospitallers of Jerusalem. These distinguished visitors came to offer Henry, then the most powerful and effective ruler in Europe, the crown of the Christian kingdom of Jerusalem, which then stood in grave danger from the infidels. The patriarch brought letters from the Pope and holy relics which included the keys of the Tower of David and of the Holy Sepulchre. These were received with great honour by the king, but, although he and his court were deeply distressed by the plight of Jerusalem, the offer of the crown was declined.

A royal wedding was celebrated at the abbey in 1359, when John of Gaunt, one of the sons of Edward III, married Blanche, daughter of the

Duke of Lancaster. Edward, his sons, and a great company of lords and ladies came to the wedding, which was celebrated with several days of feasting and jousting.

At Michaelmas 1464, at a council held at Reading Abbey, it was publicly announced that the king, Edward IV, had been secretly married since May to the Lady Elizabeth Woodville, and would not, therefore, be marrying a foreign princess as his advisors had hoped. On Michaelmas Day Elizabeth was escorted into the abbey church and honoured as Queen of England.

Other less spectacular and more businesslike events took place at Reading Abbey. During the 13th century several ecclesiastical councils were held there, attended by papal legates and representatives of the English church. In the 15th century Parliament assembled there three times, on account of the plague and other troubles in London. On these occasions the resources of the abbey and the town must have been stretched to the limit, since those attending Parliament included the king and his court, the staffs of government departments, the lords spiritual and temporal, together with their servants, and the members of the Commons with their servants. Although the king and most of the nobles could be accommodated in the abbey, other important persons would have to be entertained at the houses of the wealthier local residents, and many lesser persons would seek lodgings in the town.

The Middle Ages: Growth and Prosperity

Meanwhile the people of Reading, who had jostled in the streets to watch the great ones pass, or gossiped with the great ones' servants in shops and taverns, had been striving to win prosperity and independence for themselves.

The privileges granted by the founder had made the abbot lord of the manor of Reading, with the right to dispense justice and to control the town and its trade through officers appointed by himself. It was not long before relations between town and abbey grew strained, because the burgesses of the town claimed that they had the right to control their own affairs through their merchant guild. By the middle of the 13th century various longstanding grievances had led to bitter disputes and sometimes to open violence in the streets. The abbot's officers were accused of oppressive and unfair practices when carrying out their duties; the townsmen became obstructive; some of them waylaid the men from the abbey and beat them up. In 1253 the abbot took the case to the king's court, and there the burgesses put forward as their defence a claim that they had rights of self government going back to a time long before the abbey had been founded. They lost the case because they were unable to produce any written evidence to support their claim, but later that year they presented to the king a petition, accompanied by a handsome gift, which persuaded him to grant them a charter. This, the first of the historic charters granting privileges and powers of self-government to the borough of Reading, gave all members of the guild the right to buy and sell free from tolls or any other dues throughout the whole of England.

Armed with their charter the burgesses were able to come to terms with the abbot, and these terms were to govern relations between abbey and guild up to the time of the abbey's dissolution. The abbot agreed that the guild should continue in perpetuity, and that it should have its guildhall, twelve properties and the large meadow known as the Portmanbrook, which lay between the town and the Thames, in return for an annual rent. Each year the abbot was to choose one of the guild members to hold the office of warden of the guild, provided that he was acceptable to the other members. Every burgess was to pay the abbot an annual fee of fivepence in return for the right to trade in Reading, and the abbot was to receive part of the entry fees of all new guild members. Whenever a court of justice was held in the guildhall the warden was to deliver up the keys to the abbot's representative, and all judicial fines were payable to the abbot.

This agreement did not bring about perfect harmony between the abbey and the town, but matters were very much improved. From that time the guild became increasingly powerful and, by the beginning of the 14th century, its warden was being styled mayor.

During the second half of the 13th century national gatherings known as Parliaments began to be held, to which representatives from various English boroughs were summoned. In 1295, for the first time, Reading was asked to send representatives. In that year a writ, addressed to all county sheriffs, directed them to cause to be elected, without delay, two knights from each shire, two citizens from each city, "and from each borough two burgesses of the more discreet and able sort." Two such men were duly elected from among the burgesses of Reading and a message was sent to inform the sheriff of their names, Geoffrey de Engleys and Elias of Banbury. From that time the borough has been continuously responsible for sending representatives to Parliament.

During the medieval period Reading developed rapidly as a marketing and manufacturing centre, soon surpassing its ancient rival, Wallingford. The weekly market drew country people from miles around the town to sell their produce and to buy articles made by Reading craftsmen. In earlier times the market had been held in St Mary's Butts, but the influence and control of the abbey caused the town to develop eastwards, and the market was moved to an open space near the main gateway into the abbey. This area is still called Market Place, although in the 1970s the market was moved back to St Mary's Butts.

Fairs were held less frequently than markets, but they were among the great events of the year. The privilege of holding a fair was usually granted by the king. Henry I gave Reading the right to hold one at the feast of St Laurence (10 August); Henry II another at the feast of St James (25 July); and King John another at the feast of St Philip and St James (1 May). Merchants of all kinds, pedlars, jugglers, quacks, tricksters and customers of every degree travelled long distances to

St Mary's Church, from a print published in 1805.

attend these fairs, each of which lasted for three days in addition to the feast day of the saint.

By the end of the 12th century Reading had grown large enough to need three parish churches. The minster chuch of St Mary (to whose original function Minster Street owes its name) had in Saxon times provided clergy to minister to an area which included Tilehurst, Theale, Purley, Pangbourne, Englefield and Sulham. In the course of time resident priests were sent to those outlying villages, leaving St Mary's to serve a fast-growing congregation in Reading. The town, which had originally clustered around St Mary's Church and St Mary's Butts, began to expand to the south and east.

On the south side of the Kennet houses began to line the roads leading out of town towards London and Southampton. To serve the

31

population in this area a daughter church was built on the hillside between the two roads. It was dedicated to St Giles, the then very popular patron saint of blacksmiths, cripples and beggars. By the year 1200 St Giles' had its own graveyard, a sign that it was by that time a separate parish church.

On the eastern side of Reading another new community grew up around the abbey walls, and for these people St Laurence's Church was built beside the abbey gate. In 1196, in the time of Abbot Hugh II, St Laurence's was enlarged, and, as befitted a church so closely associated with a wealthy abbey, it became the most splendid of the three medieval parish churches.

At the other end of Friar Street (then known as New Street), another church, boasting no worldly riches, was completed about 1311. It had been built by a community of friars of the Order of St Francis of Assisi, who had come to Reading in 1233 seeking permission to establish a centre from which they could minister to the poor and the oppressed. The Grey Friars were not welcomed by the abbot, who forsaw that this rival order might challenge the influence of the abbey, but they were under royal patronage and he was obliged to let them stay.

Grudgingly he gave them a plot of low-lying, marshy ground beside the road leading to Caversham Bridge, and on this inhospitable site the friars built a church, chapter house, dormitory and refectory. They were aided generously by gifts from King Henry III of warm clothing, fuel, and timber from Windsor Forest. But the site proved impossible. It was not only unwholesomely damp but often so cut off by mud and water that the friars were unable to get to the town to carry out their work or to buy basic necessities. Fortunately, in 1282 the Archbishop of Canterbury, himself a Franciscan, intervened, and three years later obtained for them a site on higher ground at the western end of Friar Street. Here they built a new church, plain but beautiful, and large enough to accommodate the crowds who flocked to hear them preach.

The growth and prosperity of Reading in the middle ages owed much to the manufacture of woollen cloth and leather goods. Among the earliest craft guilds of the town were those for drapers, weavers, fullers and shoemakers. Other craftsmen working in cloth or leather included dyers, hatters, saddlers, skinners and glovers.

The manufacture of cloth was a national industry which had developed out of the production of fine quality wool from English sheep. Reading became a clothmaking centre because it was accessible from the wool producing areas of Hampshire, Berkshire and the Cotswolds, and it had the necessary water supply, plenty of cheap labour among the poor people of the town, and transport facilities from the town wharf to the Thames waterway and London.

Clothmaking was a complicated business involving several different processes, each carried out by specialised workers. The raw wool had to be washed, carded, spun, woven into lengths of cloth, dyed, cleaned and thickened, dried, sheared smooth, and rolled into bales. Some of the early processes could be carried out in the homes of the workers, almost the whole family taking part. It was said that poor people, whom God had blessed with many children, could so train them that by the time they were six or seven years of age they were able to earn their own bread.

The later processes were carried out by skilled craftsmen, such as weavers, fullers, dyers and shearmen. The Kennet played its essential role by contributing a plentiful supply of fast running water for the operation of the fulling mills. Here the woven cloth was beaten under water to make it shrink, giving it strength and thickness, and cleaned with fuller's earth. Water was also needed by the dyers, and Reading was fortunate in that the Kennet divided into several streams as it ran through the town.

So widespread and important an industry had to be well organised and controlled, for the continuing prosperity of the town depended upon the good reputation of its cloth. The merchant guild did its best to maintain standards by appointing wardens of individual crafts, and in 1487 its authority was confirmed by a charter granted by Henry VII. This gave the mayor responsibility for the supervision and correction of all men in Reading engaged in the making of cloth, and all trades connected with it, and for ensuring that all defective work was made good.

Another sign of the guild's authority was the wool beam with its standard weights, which stood on the town wharf under the supervision of the guildhall nearby. Although the guild had gained almost full control over the industry the abbot had the right to choose, from candidates selected by the guild, a Keeper of the Cloth Seal, whose duty was to attach a leaden seal to rolls of cloth which had been inspected and found to be up to standard.

In the 15th and 16th centuries cloth was to Reading what biscuits were to be in 19th century. John Leland, one of the first English topographers, who travelled about the country in the years between 1535 and 1543, wrote: "In the vale of the town of Reading, where the two arms of Kennet run near together, I marked divers armlets breaking out of the two streams and making medians, over which be divers bridges of wood. And these waters be very commodious for dyers, well occupied there; for the town chiefly standeth by clothing."

Dissolution and Destruction

By the time Leland rode into Reading in 1542 the monastic life of the abbey was over. The buildings remained, at that date structurally intact, although plundered and stripped of all their valuable contents. Gold and silver plate and rich hangings had been taken away for the king's use; the monks had been turned out into the world to earn livings elsewhere; the last abbot had died a martyr's death. Reading Abbey, like hundreds of other religious houses in England, had been dissolved.

The dissolution of the monasteries which took place between 1536 and 1539 was part of a complex and widespread movement towards religious reform. Long before the reign of Henry VIII people had begun to censure corruption among the clergy and the easy living standards enjoyed within the church. The church's right to the extensive landed wealth and privileges which it possessed began to be questioned. Many of its traditional ceremonies and practices came to be regarded as superstitious and idolatrous, while some of its ways of making money aroused resentment and disgust.

In many monasteries the ascetic way of life which had inspired their foundation was no longer practised very strictly by the monks. As landowners, administrators, businessmen, they had become involved in worldly affairs, but they were not serving the world as they had done in earlier centuries. Originally monasteries had provided, almost uniquely, centres of learning and education, repositories for rare and valuable manuscripts, hospitals for the sick, and shelter for travellers. Universities, schools, hospitals and inns now existed to carry out these functions. Moreover, in the world of learning, new ways of thinking were being taught, based on the study of original texts and directed towards the search for new ideals and new religious truths. The invention of the printing press in the 15th century had made books easier to produce and far more widely available, contributing to the spread of learning.

Anti-clerical opinion was strong in London and the south-east (it seems certainly to have been strong in Reading) and this made it easier for Henry VIII, motivated by his desire to divorce Queen Catherine and marry Anne Boleyn, to break away from the Church of Rome. In 1535, with the support of Parliament, he assumed the title of Supreme Head of the Church in England, and Thomas Cromwell, his secretary, was appointed Vicar-General.

As the king was badly in need of money Cromwell immediately set about discovering what wealth might be gained from the suppression of the monasteries. Commissioners were sent to all the religious houses in England to assess their value and to enquire into the way in which they were being conducted. Reading Abbey was wealthy, its income being in the region of £2,000 a year, and it was apparently well run. No tales of scandalous misconduct or corruption were reported from Reading, as they were from many other houses. Dr. John London, a canon of Windsor and Warden of New College, Oxford, who was the commissioner sent to Reading, reported to Cromwell, "The monks have a good lecture in scripture daily read in their Chapter House, both in English and Latin, to which is good resort and the Abbot is at it himself."

In 1536 Parliament passed an act providing for the suppression of all religious houses with an annual income of less than £200, and declaring that their properties belonged to the king. For the time being Reading Abbey was safe, but the days of the lesser houses were numbered.

In September 1538 Dr London carried out his work of dissolution and destruction in Reading and Caversham. On 14 September he wrote briefly to Cromwell, "Today will I go to Caversham, a mile from Reading, where is great pilgrimage, and send the image up to Your Lordship's place in London." The image was the statue of Our Lady of Caversham, which was torn from its shrine, nailed up in a box, and sent by barge to London.

In the same month he dealt with the house of Greyfriars. "Household stuff coarse;" he wrote, "what little plate and jewels there is I will send up this week. There is a great trough of lead at their well, and another in their kitchen, and the bell turret is covered with lead. Church ornaments slender. The inside of the church and windows decked with grey friars I have defaced, and yet made some money out of these things. On Monday I will pay their debts to the victuallers and rid the house of them all."

When the day came the friars, released from their vows, were provided with secular clothing and a little money and sent out into the world to earn livings as best they could. No sooner had they gone than the friary was looted by the poor people of Reading. Dr London reported indignantly to his master: "The multitude of the poverty of the town resorted thither, and all things that might be had they stole away, in so much that they had conveyed the very clappers of the bells; and saving that Mr Vachell, which made me great cheer at his house, and the mayor did assist me, they would have made no little spoil."

Thomas Vachell, M.P. for Reading and also in the service of Cromwell, assisted Dr London throughout the dissolution, and after the fall of the abbey he was appointed custodian of the abbey plate, vestments, hangings and other valuables. Vachell and the mayor were anxious to preserve the friary buildings for a special reason: the nave and aisles of the church could be adapted for use as a guild hall. For many years the guild had needed a new hall, the existing one beside the Kennet being too small and so near the common washing place of the town that it was often impossible to hear anyone speak because of the noise made by the washerwomen. With Vachell's help the mayor petitioned the king to grant the guild part of the Greyfriars' church for use as a hall and, after four years delay, the petition was granted in 1543. The rest of the church, the friary buildings, orchards, gardens and other appurtenances were sold to Robert Stanshawe, a Groom of the King's Chamber. His name is perpetuated today by Stanshawe Road.

Meanwhile, in the House of Lords, pressure had been brought to bear upon the abbots of the greater abbeys to dissolve their houses voluntarily and surrender their possessions to the king. Pensions were offered as incentives to abbots and monks, and in most places these were accepted, as they were at Berkshire's other abbey at Abingdon. Only three refused to submit: the abbots of Colchester, Glastonbury and Reading.

Hugh Cook Faringdon had been Abbot of Reading since 1520. As abbot of one of the richest abbeys in England he was a prelate of considerable power and influence and a spiritual peer. For most of his years in office he had been on friendly terms with the king, entertaining him at the abbey and exchanging gifts with him. Like many other good Catholics he had supported the king in his attempt to obtain an annulment of his marriage to Catherine, and in 1534 he had acknowledged Henry as supreme head on earth of the church in England. But his conscience would not permit him to deny the Pope's supremacy in spiritual matters. He declared that he would pray for the Pope's holiness as long as he lived, and would say mass for him once a week in the hope that the whole country might one day return to the

The execution of Hugh Cook Faringdon, the last abbot of Reading, 15 November 1539.

Church of Rome.

All attempts to persuade him to change his mind failed. In September 1539 he was arrested and sent to the Tower, and on the 19th of that month Reading Abbey was formally dissolved. In November he was brought back to Reading "to be tried and executed," as Cromwell wrote in his memoranda, showing that the verdict had been decided upon before the trial. The charge was one of high treason for denying the supremacy of the king. The abbot was allowed no defence and was declared guilty by a sworn jury composed mainly of local gentry, to many of whom he must have been well known in his years as lord of the manor. He was sentenced to the cruel death of a traitor, that of hanging, drawing and quartering. On 14 November he was dragged on a hurdle through the streets of the town to the gallows which had been set up outside the abbey gate; and there the sentence was carried out in the presence of the townspeople. With him were executed two monks, John Rugge and John Eynon, both charged with being his accomplices. Before the end of the year the abbots of Colchester and Glastonbury had suffered the same fate.

Reading Abbey was taken over for secular uses. In September the commissioners who came to dissolve it were once again entertained at Thomas Vachell's house, and in Vachell's keeping were placed all the plate and other valuables removed from the abbey for the future use of the king. Another of Cromwell's men, Sir William Penizon, was put in charge of the abbey buildings, some of which were adapted for occasional use as a royal residence. Part of the hospitium was converted into stables for the king's horses.

So matters remained until the death of Henry VIII in 1547. No sooner was the young King Edward VI on the throne than the Duke of Somerset, his uncle and the Lord Protector of the Realm, set about procuring for himself a large share of the possessions of the former abbey of Glastonbury and the lordship of the manor of Reading. Within a few months the abbey buildings had been surveyed and their value in terms of materials assessed. In 1549 the systematic destruction of the abbey church and other unwanted monastic buildings began. Lead and timber were stripped from the roofs, painted glass removed from the windows, stone pillars taken down and paving stones torn up. Huge quantities of valuable materials were loaded onto barges and taken away to London. Others were sold locally. St Mary's Church, then undergoing restoration, was partly rebuilt with stone and timber from the abbey. The churchwardens' accounts for that time contain some revealing entries:

"Paid for taking down of the choir in the abbey and
for the carriage home of the same . . . 21 loads . . . . . 10s. 6d.
Paid for the roof in the abbey . . . . £6 10s. 8d.
Paid for 21 loads of timber out of the abbey . . . . 6s. 8d.
Paid for the pillars . . . . 10s. 0d.
Paid for the door that stood in the cloister and for
stone in the church . . . . 8s. 0d.
Paid for 10 loads of stone carried out of the abbey . . 2s. 6d."

The receipts recorded on Somerset's behalf include other pathetic entries:

"Received of William Draper of London for all the
old glass £6. 13s. 4d
Received of the said William Draper for all the
images and stones standing at the high altar . . . . 46s. 8d.
Received of the Churchwardens of St Mary's
Church for the monks stalls in the choir . . . . 53s 4d.
Received of Mr Vachell for the roof of the library £6. 0s. 0d.
Received of Mr Riggs for all the cabins in the
infirmary wherein the sick monks lay . . . . £3. 0s. 0d.

Received of Thomas Mawks for the common jakeses
of the dorter .... 15s. 0d.
Received of John Redges for 3 old bedsteads, an old
table, 3 forms and an old portal .... 7s. 0d.
Received of Frances Beke for one thousand paving
tiles .... 6s. 8d.

Nothing removable can have been left within the ruined walls; and even those were used as a quarry for stone and rubble until the 19th century, when the last few remains were acquired by Reading Corporation and preserved for posterity.

Reading in the Reign of Elizabeth I

In September 1533 church bells were rung to celebrate the birth of a daughter to Henry VIII, the Princess Elizabeth. In September 1560 Elizabeth, now Queen and in the second year of her reign, set her hand to one of the most important of the royal charters granted to Reading, giving the town greater powers of self government than it had ever had before. It confirmed the charter granted by her father after the dissolution of the abbey, designating the mayor and burgesses the corporate governing body of the town, and set out at length their powers and responsibilities.

In brief, the council of the borough was to consist of nine head burgesses (including the mayor), and twelve or more secondary burgesses. Corporately they had the right to own lands and tenements and to collect rents from these for the maintenance of the borough and the administration of its affairs. They were to appoint two treasurers, two sergeants at mace and a clerk to the market. They could make and enforce byelaws for the good government of the borough and of all its tradesmen and inhabitants. They were to ensure that all weights and measures in use were accurate, and that sales of bread, wine, ale and other foods were regularly inspected and controlled. The weekly saturday market was to continue and four fairs could be held each year, from all of which the council was to receive the tolls which had formerly accrued to the abbot. They were to maintain a prison called the Counter for the safe custody of felons taken within the borough and awaiting trial, and for the punishment of other offenders. The mayor was to be a justice of the peace and was to appoint each year the necessary constables and watchmen. Finally, the mayor and burgesses were to be responsible for electing, and if need be dismissing, the Master of Reading Grammar School.

In compliment to the Queen the borough coat of arms, which had formerly borne a king's head surrounded by four men's heads, perhaps representing the merchant guild, was changed to one bearing the head of a queen and four maidens.

The charter made special mention of the state of the bridges in and around the town. Nineteen of them were described as "very ruinous", and "in great decay from default of repairs and amendments . . . so that no passage can be made over the same bridges without great danger as well of our subjects as of horses, oxen and animals." Access to and from the town was thereby diminished and had led to the decay of many houses and poverty among the inhabitants. For the repair of the bridges the Queen gave permission for 30 oak trees to be taken from the manor of Whitley and 200 loads of stones and other materials from Reading Abbey. The council was to be responsible for the future repair and maintenance of the bridges.

The decision made some twenty years earlier to use part of the former Greyfriars Church as a town hall had, apparently, not proved a happy one. Perhaps the church was too cold and uncomfortable for such a purpose. At any rate the council had evidently sought, and Elizabeth now granted, permission to use or dispose of the building in any other way they pleased. By 1578 it was in use as a "hospital" for poor people, who were expected to work to help pay for their keep; and in 1590 the council converted part of it into a house of correction for the punishment of idle and vagrant persons.

The council moved to a new hall which they created by building an upper floor into the lofty refectory of the former abbey hospitium, the ground floor of which had been used since about 1486 as the schoolroom of Reading School. This thrifty move brought the council to the site on which two later town halls were to be built, and which was to be the home of local government in Reading for the next 400 years.

In Elizabeth's reign Reading was still very small and compact, roughly triangular in shape, and extending from the line of Friar Street in the north to the junction of Silver Street and Southampton Street in the south. The area of greatest density lay on the north side of the Kennet, and here was the busiest part of the town. Here the houses with their jettied storeys and swinging signboards crowded close together along the narrow streets. Here in their dark little shops craftsmen such as shoemakers, glovers, tailors, saddlers, loriners and many others made as well as sold their goods, opening up each morning simply by letting down the wooden window shutters which also did duty as counters. Some of the street names, such as Hosiers' Lane, indicated the principal trade that was carried on there. Fish Row and Butcher Row divided what is now the eastern end of Broad Street, while Shoemakers' Row occupied the eastern side of the Market Place.

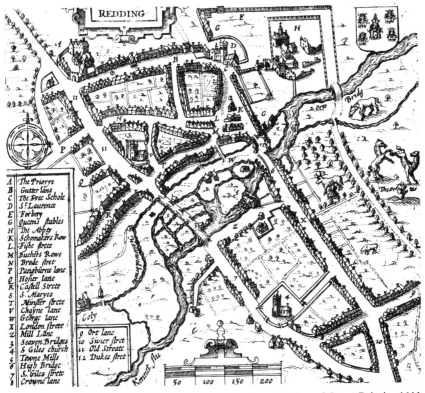

The earliest map of Reading, published in John Speed's atlas of Great Britain, 1611.

Gutter Lane no doubt picturesquely described the street in which slaughter houses were situated; it is now Cross Street.

To the east of High Bridge was the town wharf, where goods could be unloaded and carried within a few minutes up to the market stalls and shops. Some trading also took place on the wharf. In 1591 the council agreed that "all such kind of boatmen as do use this town shall bring all kind of fish which they do bring into the Cheese Row, alias Fish Row, except it be all shellfish, and as for roots, onions and such like, they may sell them on their boat, paying toll therefore." Owing to the rough and unreliable state of the roads, and the consequent difficulties of land transport, rivers were still the main routes for the carriage of heavy and bulky goods.

To the west of High Bridge stood the former Guild, or Yield Hall, by that time leased to private tenants. From the back of it a lane called George Lane (now Yield Hall Lane) ran up to the George Inn, to which in former times the guild members had doubtless repaired for more convivial meetings. The George was already one of the town's busiest inns. Others were The Bear, The Bell, The Rose, The Star, The Hind Head and The Cardinal's Hat. Behind all these, as behind many houses, accommodation had to be provided for horses, and most street frontages concealed a close-knit patchwork of stables, yards and outhouses.

In the Market Place stood the stocks and pillory, where many a wretched offender suffered public ridicule as well as cruel punishment. At the top of the Market Place was the town prison, known as the Counter or Compter. This was housed over the archway of the former Compter Gateway to the abbey, and had formerly been the Abbot's prison, where offenders from within the abbey or from the town had been confined. The gateway spanned The Forbury from St Lawrence's Church to the Compter House, where the gaoler lived, on the opposite corner of the Market Place.

On the southern side of the Kennet the newer part of Reading was less congested, most of the buildings being strung out along the two main streets. London Street was a wide thoroughfare lined with houses, many of them backing onto spacious gardens. Then as now it linked up with the main road to London, in those days the only eastbound route out of Reading, for Kings and Queens Roads were not constructed until the 19th century. Southampton Street was not so built up as London Street. On its western side fields sloped down to the Kennet and to a rough, wooded area called Cattell's Grove (now Katesgrove). But this street was always a busy highway and a steady flow of people, horses, farm animals and carts plodded, lurched and trundled over the Seven Bridges which linked it with the heart of the town. These ancient bridges across the Kennet streams were soon to be reduced in number (perhaps a council economy measure) for, although the Seven Bridges were among those mentioned in Elizabeth's charter as in need of repair, only five were shown on John Speed's map of Reading published in 1611, while modern Bridge Street crosses only one bridge.

On the western side of town Castle Street, already lined with houses and inns for some distance up the hill, carried the main road to the west of England which was to become the famous Bath Road of the coaching era. Even in the 16th century there was no sign of a castle to justify the name of Castle Street, and no trace or record of one has ever been found.

Travellers for Oxford then went northwards over Caversham Bridge, reached by way of Caversham Lane, an exposed and often waterlogged road requiring several small bridges to carry it over the brooks which meandered through the low-lying fields between the town and the river. The Oxford Road leading westwards from Reading in modern times was then known only as Pangbourne Lane.

Now that the abbey was in ruins the three principal buildings in the town were the parish churches. These had been left untouched at the time of the dissolution, except that space had to be found for the royal arms which were ordered to be set up in all churches as a token of the king's supremacy. In the reign of Edward VI, when the new Protestant forms of worship were introduced, the churches were stripped of everything which savoured of idolatry. In St Laurence's all the richly coloured window glass was removed and replaced by plain glass; paintings and frescoes were defaced and covered over with whitewash; altars, images, statues, crosses, censers, copes, vestments and plate were taken away. St Giles' suffered a similar fate. The churchwardens' accounts recorded payments for such alterations as "digging down of the altars in the church and for carrying away of the rubble", and "for making of the table in the choir". Other revealing entries show how the organist's wages fell from about £40 a year to a mere £2, owing to the reduction in the number of services and in the use of music.

In spite of the brief return to Catholicism in the reign of Mary the churches were never fully restored to their former state. In Elizabeth's reign the Church of England, with the Queen as Supreme Head, became firmly established. The great majority of the population welcomed the plainer church services, all in English, and the less elaborately decorated church interiors.

Throughout her long reign Elizabeth travelled frequently to the more accessible parts of her kingdom. She came to Reading several times, and lodged at the accommodation which had been maintained for her in the abbey precincts. On most occasions she attended divine service at St Laurence's, where a special seat, screened by an arras hanging, was prepared for her in the chancel. The church was made brighter and sweeter with fresh flowers and rushes, the bells rang out and were answered by the bells of St Mary's and St Giles'. Some of the streets in the town centre were swept clean — an unusual occurrence.

The Queen did what she could to encourage industry in Reading, as in other towns in her realm. Traditionally she is believed to have promoted a new industry here, that of silk weaving, by a gift of mulberry trees for the cultivation of silk worms. Silk weaving became an important industry in Reading in the 17th and 18th centuries.

In her reign clothmaking was still the major industry, although it had already begun to decline. Among other indications that business was less profitable than it had been were the clothiers' complaints that they were so hedged about with rules and regulations that they were ready to give up the industry, no matter how many livelihoods depended upon it. Searchers of cloth were empowered by the mayor to enter the clothiers' workrooms and inspect their cloth for faults. An officer called the alnager had the right of entry in order to measure the cloth and attach official seals to approved lengths, for which service he charged a fee of fourpence for the Queen's seal and a penny for the town seal.

Such controls were necessary, for among the many craftsmen engaged in the industry there were inevitably a few black sheep. Illegal practices included the use of inaccurate measures and the stretching of lengths of cloth while they were drying by means of gins, levers and ropes. Since the alnager was so unwelcome at certain houses all clothiers were ordered, in 1597, to take their cloth to a house in the middle of the town, so that the alnager could measure it there. Many clothiers refused to obey this order, claiming that it had always been their custom to bale their cloth, tack a fourpenny piece to it for the Queen's seal, and deliver it to the wharf to await despatch by boat to London. They also complained that the alnager charged more than his legal fees and had sometimes used violence in the execution of his duty. On one occasion the mayor, who happened to be crossing High Bridge, saw an angry crowd surrounding the alnager, who had just cut into two a length of cloth which he claimed was faulty. The mayor had to intervene to keep the peace.

Indirectly, the clothing trade conferred lasting benefits on Reading in the shape of charities founded by three famous men whose fathers were clothiers in Reading.

Sir Thomas White was born in Reading in 1492 and, at the age of twelve, was placed in an apprenticeship in London. His career as a merchant tailor was so successful that he was made Sheriff of London in the reign of Edward VI and Lord Mayor in the reign of Mary, by whom he was knighted. He founded St John's College, Oxford, and endowed schools in various towns with scholarships to the college. Two White scholarships were given to Reading School. He died in 1566.

William Laud was born in 1573 in a house on the north side of Broad Street. He was sent to Reading School and, at the age of 16, to St John's College where he was one of the earliest White Scholars. In due course he was made a Fellow of St John's and later its President. His learning took him far from the clothing trade into the highest ranks of the Church. In 1633 Charles I made him Archbishop of Canterbury.

Laud was a generous benefactor to Oxford University and to the town of his birth. He was instrumental in obtaining for Reading, in 1638, a charter which remained the governing instrument of the town until 1835. In 1640 he gave the Corporation lands to the value of £200 a year, and directed that after his death £120 was to be used either to help apprentice poor boys or to give poor girls a marriage portion. The rest of the money was to be divided between the vicar of St Laurence's Church, where Laud had been christened, and the master of Reading School.

John Kendrick was born in Reading in 1573, the son of a clothier who had a prosperous business in Minster Street. Like his contemporary, William Laud, he was educated at Reading School and at St John's College, but around 1595 he went to London to make his fortune in the clothing trade. When he died in 1624 he was worth more than £30,000. To Reading Corporation he left a large sum of money for the purpose of providing a workhouse where the poor people of Reading might be employed in the clothing industry. His charity, after a devious and unfortunate history, was eventually to endow Kendrick School.

A fourth famous benefactor was John Blagrave, not the son of a clothier but a member of the wealthy Blagrave family who owned considerable estates around Reading. John Blagrave lived at Southcote Lodge and devoted much of his life to the study of mathematics. In 1585 he published a book entitled *The Mathematical Jewel*. This was followed by three other scientific books, winning him a high reputation among scholars. He was esteemed as 'the flower of mathematicians of his age'.

He died in 1611, leaving in his will £10 a year to be used by Reading Corporation for the benefit of poor maid servants. On Good Friday

Part of the monument in St Laurence's Church to John Blagrave, showing the famous mathematician holding a globe and a quadrant.

each year £6 13s 4d was to be awarded as a marriage portion to a poor maid servant who could show that she had served well for at least five years. There were to be three candidates each year, if possible one from each parish, and every fifth year one of the maids was to be chosen from Southcote. The rest of the money was to go to the poor. In addition he left money to build an arcade at the side of St Laurence's Church and to improve the Market Place. He was buried in St Laurence's, where an unusual monument may be seen, showing him surrounded by mathematical and allegorical figures.

The Poor and
The Oracle

By the end of Elizabeth's reign responsibility for the poor had become one of the major problems facing the borough council. Up to the time of the Dissolution the poor had been the responsibility of the church; the abbey had provided alms, food and medical care; the humble Grey Friars had devoted much of their lives to the relief of poor and sick people in the town. When religious houses such as these had been suppressed all over the country responsibility for the poor fell upon the State, which decided to transfer it to the parish authorities.

In 1572 an Act of Parliament laid down that there should be overseers in each parish responsible for collecting alms for the relief of the poor and for seeing that idle rogues, vagabonds and other troublesome persons were set to some useful work. In 1597 another act was passed saying that the overseers were to be appointed by Justices and defining their duties more clearly. A third act passed in 1601 was the foundation of local poor law administration for over 200 years. It placed on the overseers the duty of maintaining the poor and setting them to work, and laid down that they were to be financed by local taxes, or poor rates, which were to be properly administered by locally appointed officers and audited by local magistrates.

These Acts were the spurs which led to the council's decision to convert the former Greyfriars Church into a combined hospital for the poor, workhouse, and house of correction for the borough. This arrangement continued throughout the 17th century, and it was not until the 18th century that a separate workhouse was provided in each parish. The three parishes were equally responsible for the borough workhouse, the council having decided that six honest men, two from each parish, should be appointed each year as masters and governors.

The council raised some of the necessary money by levying taxes, charging only those who were considered able to pay, but each parish was expected to contribute alms, and grants were also available from local charities and private benefactors. The money was spent in various ways. The ancient workhouse building was often in need of repair; tools and materials such as hemp and flax had to be purchased to keep the poor employed; food and other necessities had to be provided for the sick, aged and impotent in the hospital; salaries had to be paid to officers performing special duties, such as supervising the hospital or seeing that able-bodied but persistently idle rogues in the house of correction were properly whipped. Outside the workhouse "outdoor relief" was given to some of the deserving poor living in the town, while housewives who agreed to board homeless children were entitled to reimbursement. In 1623 the total expenditure of the overseers in the three parishes amounted to £333, of which more than half went on outdoor relief.

Income from charity was often used to help particularly bad cases of illness or destitution; 16 shillings and 8 pence was spent on Thomas Trowe, a very sick man in the workhouse, and "poor blind Robin" was given 5 shillings' worth of clothes.

A few people tried to take unfair advantage of the system, but the council dealt firmly with these. When one of the overseers of St Mary's reported that a certain Justinian Edmundes had four or five children which he left to the charge of the parish while he spent wastefully the money which he earned, the council ordered that Justinian must in future pay two shillings to the overseers every Saturday for the support of his children, and that if he failed to pay in any week he was to be set to work in the house of correction.

Beggars and other indigent travellers were not encouraged to linger in Reading. In 1625 the council decided that the beadles should regularly collect up all the beggars in the streets and bring them before a magistrate, who would commit them to the house of correction.

Attempts to reform idle and unruly persons by means of corporal punishment were not very successful, and the rising cost of whippings caused the council some concern. In 1624, 13 shillings and 4 pence was paid to two men for whipping rogues in the house of correction. Two years later three Constables claimed repayment of 41 shillings and 4 pence laid out for whippings, but the Council would agree to pay only 30 shillings towards this claim. After further deliberation it was decided that the Town Crier should henceforth be at the command of the Constables and the Overseers of the house of correction, to whip and punish offenders according to their instructions, and that he should not be paid by the Constables but should have a regular quarterly payment of 2 shillings and 6 pence from the Mayor.

In spite of all the Council's efforts the problem of the poor grew worse year by year. The number of unemployed in the town increased, and the Council was only too well aware that the major cause of the increase was the decline of the once wealthy clothmaking industry. From the early years of the century there had been complaints that many humble workers, such as spinners and carders, who had depended upon the clothiers for their livings were now unable to find employment. The Council tried to remedy the situation by ordering the clothiers to find work for as many as possible of these unfortunate people, and forbade them to send work out to country people while there were so many unemployed in the town. In 1623 clothiers' overseers were appointed in each parish to assist the Churchwardens and the Overseers of the Poor to find places for the unemployed. The hard-pressed clothiers protested that trade was so bad that they were quite unable to take on any more workers. Sales of Reading cloth were falling because of unfair competition from clothiers in the north of England, who, by special privilege, paid less customs duty and could afford to manufacture more coloured cloth, whereas Reading clothiers made mostly white cloth. The Council summoned the clothiers to a meeting "to show the causes of the decay of their trade, and why they cannot set the poor on work as they have done, but suffer them to cry and complain for lack of work."

What was said at that meeting was not recorded, but no solution to the problem was found, and when help came at last it was from another source and, sadly, was too late.

On 30 December 1624 the death took place at his house in London of John Kendrick, a wealthy clothier and Freeman of the Worshipful Company of Drapers. He left a fortune of over £30,000 which, having no children, he bestowed upon various charitable causes. Mindful of the fact that he had made his fortune in the clothing trade and in the export of cloth overseas, several of his bequests were designed to encourage this industry. Since his brother William still carried on the Kendrick family business in Minster Street, and had served for many years on the Borough Council, John was well aware how bad the situation was both in Reading and in the neighbouring town of Newbury. Two of his most generous bequests were £7,500 to the Mayor and Burgesses of Reading and £4,000 to the Mayor and Burgesses of Newbury. Each town was to use part of the money to provide a house, "fit and commodious for setting of the poor on work therein, with a fair garden adjoining", and the remainder as a common

John Kendrick, founder of the Oracle workhouse for poor clothiers.

stock of capital available for loan to clothiers to help improve and expand the industry. In each case there was a proviso that, should the Mayor and Burgesses fail to carry out his wishes, or misemploy the money in any way, the entire sum should be forfeited, Newbury's to Reading and Reading's to Christ's Hospital in London.

To his brother William, John left £2,000 to be divided between him and his children. This was not over-generous compared with his other bequests, but William found another way of benefiting from John's will. His house in Minster Street, in which he carried on the clothmaking business established by his father some fifty years before, was very suitable for conversion into the workhouse which the council was required to provide under the terms of John Kendrick's will. It was conveniently situated in one of the busiest thoroughfares in the town, and there was ample space to extend the workshops so that more people could be employed. He himself was nearing fifty and fairly prosperous. It would be pleasant to be able to retire.

In 1625 William agreed to sell to the Council, for the sum of £2,000, "all his dwelling-house and out-houses, backsides and gardens, as well freehold as leasehold, with all the glass, wainscot, doors, locks and keys in and about the premises, and also all his farm and lands, tenements and hereditaments in North Street and Tilehurst". Some

52

The entrance to the Oracle in Minster Street, from a print published in 1802.

months later the council agreed to buy all William's equipment and goods belonging to the clothing trade which might be of use to them, when he moved out of his house.

After a long delay the legal and financial arrangements were completed in February 1627, and the council, by that time under some pressure from the poor and unemployed, promptly ordered the work of enlargement and conversion to begin. The local brickmaking industry benefited. William Brockman, brickmaker of Tilehurst, contracted to supply 200,000 serviceable bricks and 20,000 large and serviceable tiles at 12 shillings and 6 pence per thousand each, and as much lime and sand as should be required.

The building was completed by Midsummer 1628, when William Kendrick moved out and his brother John Kendrick's workhouse finally came into being. For an undiscovered reason it became known by the attractive but mysterious name of The Oracle. It consisted of a range of workshops surrounding a spacious courtyard, through which ran the Holy Brook, and the whole establishment covered an area of about two acres. The former Kendrick family house remained on the Minster Street side, but the main entrance to The Oracle was through an imposing arched gateway facing westwards into Gun Street. On the massive wooden gates were carved the initials J.K. and the date 1628.

John Kendrick's scheme was not rewarded with the success it so well deserved. The capital he had entrusted to the town was not wisely used. The poor did not benefit as much as they should have done from the facilities at The Oracle. The clothing trade continued to decline and, within twenty years, the Civil Wars had put an end to any real hope of its recovery. The Oracle was used for various purposes during the following 200 years but, by the middle of the 19th century, it was a useless ruin. Christ's Hospital was able to prove that John Kendrick's will had not been properly carried out, in Reading or Newbury, and claimed the greater part of both bequests. In 1850 The Oracle was demolished.

William Kendrick purchased a small estate at Whitley, where he was able to spend the remainder of his days away from the noise and bustle of the town and the workshop. He founded five almshouses in Silver Street for people who were aged and past work. He died in 1635 and was buried in St Mary's Church, where a monument on the chancel wall shows him and his wife, Jane, dressed in their sober Sunday best, kneeling in prayer.

Visitations of the Plague

A recurrent problem facing the town council in the 17th century was the plague, which broke out every few years and was particularly bad in 1608, 1625 and 1638.

The poorer parts of Reading had become unhealthily overcrowded, many families being crammed into ramshackle tenement houses and living in conditions which were known to encourage the spread of infection. But even in the better parts of the town public health measures were almost non-existent, for it was common practice for all householders to throw their garbage into the rivers or into the gutters which ran down every street and alleyway. The council had begun to employ a regular scavenger, but his duties were confined to cleaning the streets immediately around the Market Place. Elsewhere the scavenging was done, unsystematically and no doubt selectively, by stray dogs, cats, pigs and rats. Smoke and soot blown down from domestic chimneys contributed to the foulness of the atmosphere and, not surprisingly, many people believed that the plague infection was airborne. During a severe outbreak those who were able to do so fled into the purer air of the country.

Since the true carrier of the plague, the black rat, was unrecognised and no effective medical treatment was available, the council could deal with outbreaks only by isolating the sufferers and trying to prevent outsiders from bringing further infection into the town. Searchers were employed to examine corpses and, if death from plague was confirmed, the stricken families might be shut up in their houses, and other suspected cases removed to a crude isolation hospital, known as the pest house, in Conduit Close, off Whitley Street. Isolation lasted about five weeks, during which time watchmen delivered food to the confined families, and made sure that they did not escape or make contact with the outside world. The council levied taxes as necessary to pay for these services. Meanwhile trade suffered badly because of restrictions placed on goods and travellers coming into the town, and because people were reluctant to mingle with their fellow men and walked warily about the streets, muffling their faces in scarves and handkerchiefs.

By 1625 the council had established a regular procedure for coping with the plague and took action as soon as an outbreak was suspected. The first warning came at the beginning of July, when a child in John Parre's house was reported to have died "full of blue spots". A watchman was immediately sworn in to watch Parre's house and to take the household food and other necessities. A few days later two widows, Mary Jerome and Anne Lovejoy, were sworn to act as searchers of the bodies of all those who died within the borough, and to report and certify, of their knowledge, of what disease they had died. For this dangerous and gruesome work they were paid a relatively high wage of four shillings a week.

In spite of the plague it was agreed that the assizes should be held in Reading later that month, and the council made preparations for the accommodation of the judges and their clerks, servants and horses. The judges were to stay at the house of Mr Thomas Turnour, one of the senior members of the council, at no cost to himself, the clerks and servants at other private houses, and the horses at Christopher Kenton's stables or at the Hind Head Inn.

As the plague was rife in London further precautions were taken against the spread of infection from that source. Boatmen who plied regularly between the city wharves and Reading were an obvious danger, and Master Boatmen John Nashe, Symon Dye and Henry Crosse were summoned to the council chamber and strictly forbidden to bring any passengers or goods into the town. If they did so their own houses would be shut up immediately.

The townspeople for their part did not welcome the outsiders who were allowed to stay in the town for the assizes, and although the judges were well entertained at Mr Turnour's house the lesser mortals were given a cold reception at local inns. This attitude was perhaps justified, for the plague was spreading. At the end of July two more huts for the confinement of the sick were built at Conduit Close, and the council had to pay out £5 for these and for a coffin to bury the dead. It was agreed that a further £20 must be raised by taxation to pay the continuing costs of the outbreak. Another searcher was sworn in to help with the inspection of corpses.

A few days later the council ordered that if any inhabitant, during the time of the plague, received into his house any person, goods or merchandise that came from London, he was to be shut up in his house for a month and maintained at his own expense. This order was made necessary because certain people persisted in receiving wares from London, "more respecting their private gain and profit than the public calamity". On 30 August, the plague still being severe in many parts of the country, the council discussed directions sent from the King concerning the welfare of the poor who were afflicted with the plague. It was agreed that all alms money collected on Wednesday each week should be distributed among the poor who were shut up in their houses. At the same meeting the council decided that there should be more watchmen employed to watch the houses of infected and suspected persons, and also to watch the pest house and to keep suspected persons out of the town. The mayor was to appoint men to patrol each parish in order to ensure that the watchmen did not fail to do their duty.

On the first day of September the council met to elect a new mayor, Mr Roger Knight, one of whose first tasks was to deal with a complaint against a certain "Mr Smith, a foreigner", who was said to be bringing goods from London into the town and selling them, much to the disadvantage of the local tradesmen.

But the worst of the outbreak was over. On 5 September two men who had been shut up in their houses for over five weeks were set at liberty. On the 19th permission was granted to a tradesman to collect a load of salt, provided he washed his sacks well at the wharf. Similarly Edward Bagley was to have his fish, first washing it well at the wharf, and Robert Stevens his soap, first washing his barrels at the wharf.

On the 23rd a joyful Mr Kenton was allowed to take home his son out of the Conduit Close, with instructions to burn his clothes and buy him new ones; and Richard Booth, a shoemaker, having been well for a month since his sickness was allowed to resume work.

Another visitation was over, and life returned to normal.

The Civil War

Although most of the famous battles in the war between King and Parliament were fought in other parts of the country, Berkshire suffered as badly as any, and worse than many, counties. Caught between the Royalist forces at Oxford and the Parliamentary forces in London, Berkshire people had to endure for several years the movements of troops across their lands, occasional battles and bloody skirmishes, soldiers billeted in their towns and villages, their property destroyed, their horses, cattle and corn stolen, and their menfolk pressed into military service. On top of all this both King and Parliament demanded regular supplies of money and provisions to support their armies.

The situation was the more unhappy because the war was no simple matter of fighting a common enemy. The complex issues at stake, involving politics, religion, taxation, the rights of the King and the rights of the people, divided the inhabitants of town and village, and even members of the same family. In Reading conflicting loyalties divided the council. Some members refused to attend meetings and suffered imprisonment and heavy fines as a penalty for their absence.

Among local landowning families the Vachells of Coley were divided, Thomas being a Royalist and Tanfield a Parliamentarian. Anthony Blagrave of Bulmershe Court was a Royalist; Daniel Blagrave of Southcote was a Parliamentarian and, eventually, one of the regicides. The Knollys of Battle Manor supported Parliament; the old Catholic families, such as the Blounts of Mapledurham and the Englefields of Whiteknights, were loyal to the King.

The first full battle of the war was fought at Edgehill in Warwickshire on 23 October 1642. The better trained and equipped Royalist forces won the way, but not so decisively as to encourage the King to advance immediately on London. A few days after the battle he led his army into Oxford, which was to be his capital throughout the war, although the sympathies of many of the townspeople lay with

Parliament.

Meanwhile Reading had been garrisoned for Parliament by Henry Marten, M.P. for the county, whose estates were in north Berkshire and who had raised his own regiment of horse for the defence of the Parliamentary cause. His performance at Reading, however, was not impressive. The town was unfortified and, in the opinion of the town council, in great danger "by reason of the Cavaliers abroad." Scouts were sent out daily to look for signs of the enemy, and watchmen were posted day and night. At the end of October conflicting rumours concerning the outcome of the battle at Edgehill threw the townspeople into confusion, and when, on 1 November, a party of Royalist horse was seen approaching the outskirts, Marten hastily abandoned the town.

Three days later it was occupied by the Royalist army, the King being welcomed by the many leading townsmen who were loyal to him; many who were not had left in the wake of Henry Marten. The King remained a few days only in Reading, and then advanced with his army upon London. But there he met with such strong opposition from the Parliamentary forces and from the citizens, who turned out in their thousands to defend their city, that he was obliged to withdraw. On 19 November he re-entered Reading, where the church bells rang out to celebrate his return.

Reading was to remain in Royalist hands for some time, and was the largest garrison town outside Oxford, over 3,000 soldiers being quartered in and around it. The King soon returned to Oxford, leaving the town council to worry about how to raise the necessary money "to pay those great charges which are now laid upon the Borough concerning cloth, apparel, victuals and other things for His Majesty's army." A rate of tax was duly agreed upon and collectors were appointed. The council could not have guessed that, for the next few years, they would meet to discuss little else but the levying of taxes, the raising of loans, the problems (which turned out to be impossibilities) of persuading the King to repay the loans, the increasing impoverishment of the town, and the bankruptcy of some of its leading citizens who had rashly advanced money in the Royal cause.

At the end of November 1642 the town was ordered to contribute £102 towards the provision of horsemeat for the King's army, to be paid "on Friday next". Hardly had this matter been dealt with than the Mayor and Aldermen hastened to wait upon the newly appointed Governor of the town, Sir Arthur Aston, in order to discuss with him how they could raise the £500 a week which the King was then demanding. Almost immediately another tax had to be levied to pay for wood and coal for fires in the various guardhouses in the town. Such taxes were to be levied many times and were rigorously enforced; people who refused to pay were reported to the Governor.

During January 1643 two loans of £2,000 each were demanded by the King. On receiving the demand for the second loan the council decided to petition the King to be excused, pleading that they were unable to pay because of the great burdens and losses they had already suffered. They were not excused. Somehow the money had to be raised. Alderman Thomas Harrison, a wealthy brewer, loaned the council £600 for six months, on security of some of the council's property. He was never repaid.

The King controlled most of north Berkshire. Two regiments of horse were stationed at Abingdon, which commanded an important bridge across the Thames. At Wallingford, Royalists fortified the ancient castle and two heavy cannon were positioned in the town. Warrants were sent out for all arms to be brought to the castle, and all local ovens were ordered to be employed in baking biscuits for the soldiers' rations.

Newbury, on the other hand, was strongly sympathetic to the Parliamentary cause and, early in the war, had craftily discouraged the approach of Royalist scouts by spreading a rumour that the plague was rife in the town. At the same time Parliamentary soldiers were invited to enter and Newbury remained loyal to Parliament throughout the war.

Windsor, too, was for Parliament. Strict forest laws, enclosures and prosecutions for poaching had bred longstanding grievances against the Crown. Town and castle were held by a strong Parliamentary garrison, while the Great Park and Forest were used as training grounds for Parliamentary soldiers. Much of east Berkshire escaped payment of the crippling taxes which were collected on behalf of the King in Reading and other parts of the county, but the countryside was, nevertheless, preyed on by soldiers of both sides. Cattle, horses, sheep and corn were taken by force. At Wargrave some villagers, with the help of Windsor troopers, prevented Royalists from taking away five cartloads of wheat and 150 sheep. At Wokingham soldiers from the Reading garrison ordered the townspeople to fill eight carts with firewood and bedding. When they failed to carry out the order four houses were destroyed in reprisal and the occupiers told to take themselves to Windsor. The people of Twyford complained bitterly to Parliament that their property was pillaged almost every day by soldiers of one side or the other. The wanton destruction of bridges, barge ferries and mills along the Thames, Loddon and Kennet further disrupted trade, communications and food supplies.

Spies sent out by Sir Samuel Luke, Scout Master General to the Earl of Essex, reported from Reading that the people were anxiously awaiting deliverance from the burden of Royalist occupation, and would be willing to risk their lives to help Parliamentary forces take the town. Sir Arthur Aston the Governor, was a Catholic and a strict disciplinarian, as unpopular with his men as with the civilians. In February 1643 a spy reported to Luke that he was in the habit of dining out at the houses of the Catholic Sir Charles Blount at Mapledurham and Anthony Englefield at Whiteknights. It might be possible to kidnap him on his journey to either place, and then take the town by surprise. But Royalist intelligence was equally efficient, and Aston was warned of the plan.

During his governorship Reading had been fortified. A line of ditches and ramparts enclosed the town, except at points where the Kennet provided sufficient defence. Earthen redoubts were built at the top of Castle Hill, guarding the Newbury road, at the western end of Friar Street, at the Abbey (now Blake's) Bridge, and at the top of Silver Street. The approaches from north and south were further guarded by fortified outposts on Whitley Hill and on the north side of Caversham Bridge. In the Forbury earthworks were constructed which involved blowing up part of the nave of Reading Abbey church. The stones were used to strengthen the defences. Cannon were placed at several strategic points in the town; council properties such as The Oracle and the house of correction were taken over for use as guardhouses; sacks of wool were commandeered to protect the defenders firing upon the enemy. Fodder and food supplies were brought daily into the town, but trade with London was prohibited by royal ordinance.

These preparations were put to the test in April 1643, when Reading was besieged by Parliamentary forces commanded by the Earl of Essex.

The Siege of Reading, 15-25 April 1643

In January 1643 Parliamentary forces under the Earl of Essex carried out a surprise attack on Henley, driving out the Royalists and taking possession of the town. It was widely believed on both sides that Essex' next objective would be Oxford. But Old Robin, as he was known to his men, was an experienced and cautious tactician. On 15 April, having marched by devious wooded, hilly ways through south Oxfordshire, he wheeled suddenly to the south and drew up his army on Caversham Heights, overlooking Reading. He had with him about 15,000 foot and 3,000 horse.

Inside the town Sir Arthur Aston commanded a mere 3,000 foot and 300 horse, but, on being summoned to surrender, he replied resolutely that he would keep the town or starve in it.

The next day the bombardment of the town began, the defenders replying fiercely with musket-shot and cannon-fire. Essex sent part of his forces to subdue Royalist fortifications at Mapledurham House and on Caversham Heights, and then directed his attack upon the Royalist defences around St Peter's Church, which guarded the way to the bridge. The church, battered by cannon-balls until its north side was in ruins and its spire knocked down, was soon untenable, and in spite of some rather half-hearted sallies from the town the Royalists were overwhelmed. By evening Essex' army had swept across Caversham Bridge and encamped in the fields on the Berkshire side of the river. All that night his men laboured at digging trenches and placing artillery, so that by morning the whole of the western side of Reading, from the Thames to the Kennet, and including the main road to Newbury, was controlled by Parliamentary forces. Essex set up his headquarters at the Blagraves' house at Southcote.

Throughout Monday 17 April the town was bombarded again, the Parliamentary soldiers continuing their work in the trenches by day and night, and gradually advancing their lines nearer to the town. There was a great deal of shooting from both sides, but few casualties.

Southcote Manor House, believed to have been the headquarters of the Earl of Essex during the Siege of Reading, April 1643. This photograph was taken shortly before the house was demolished in 1921.

On 18 April Essex had cause to regret that, as a security measure, he had ordered part of Caversham Bridge to be broken down. During the morning Royalist forces were seen riding eastwards across Caversham Heights and it was learned afterwards that, on reaching the Thames at Sonning, they had loaded 600 musketeers and a large supply of ammunition into boats and sent them upstream into the Kennet, and so safely into Reading. Essex could do nothing to prevent them.

The next day a rumour spread that Sir Arthur Aston had been killed, but this was later corrected by the news that he had been struck on the head by a falling tile and badly injured. His place as Governor was taken by his second-in-command, Colonel Richard Fielding. On the same day Essex welcomed the arrival of Lord Grey with another 3,000 foot soldiers, nearly 500 horse and three more pieces of heavy artillery. With their help he hoped to surround the town, guarding the Thames from Caversham to Sonning, and entrenching on the eastern side.

Unfortunately most of the new arrivals turned out to be raw recruits who fled in disorder before a sudden attack from the town. Essex had to send two seasoned foot regiments and five troops of horse to support them.

The bombardment of the town continued. Essex was now concentrating on its southernmost point, where, on Whitley Hill, just outside the bulwarks crossing Southampton Street and Silver Street, stood a strongly fortified outpost known as Harrison's Barn. It belonged to Thomas Harrison, the wealthy brewer who ventured so much in the cause of his King. At night Essex' men advanced their batteries on the western side until they were within pistol shot of the barn; it was planned that Lord Grey's forces would approach it similarly from the east. The southern end of Reading now came under heavy fire; St Giles' Church was badly damaged, and tradition says that its spire received a direct hit which sent it crashing to the ground.

Meanwhile Colonel Fielding had sent a message to the King at Oxford saying that he could not hold out much longer. A relief force was mustered, a summons sent to Prince Rupert, who was successfully storming Lichfield, to join him as soon as possible, and the King set out for Reading. A message was sent on ahead that supplies of powder and ammunition were on the way, and that it was a matter of urgency to warn Fielding to expect them. During the night of 22 April a man named Flower, a servant to Sir Lewis Dives, made his way through the Parliamentary lines at Caversham, swam the river and successfully delivered the message. But on the way back Flower was captured as he climbed out of the water and made to reveal the Royalist plan.

Essex sent a strong cavalry force towards Oxford, with instructions to harry and delay the Royalist advance. A smaller party was sent to ambush the supplies at Caversham. Thus, when the Royalists arrived with the ammunition they found their enemies lying in wait for them and were forced to retreat.

The Parliamentary cavalry riding northwards met up with several hundred Royalist horse at Dorchester. There, in the narrow, twisting streets, fierce and bloody fighting took place and the King's troops were routed. Essex' men claimed that over 100 Royalists were killed. They returned to Reading in triumph, bringing many prisoners and some captured Royalist colours, the sight of which must have increased the alarm and despondency of the besieged forces.

At Reading there had been little activity that day. A spy sent to blow up Essex' powder magazine was caught and hanged. There were

St Giles' Church, from a print published in 1802. The steeple is believed to have been badly damaged during the Siege of Reading. The present spire was added in 1872-3.

rumours that food supplies were running so short in the town that the besieged were eating horse-flesh; Essex' soldiers joked that the Royalist cavalry had tried to escape with their horses, but had been prevented by the foot regiments.

On 24 April, about noon, there was a sudden desperate attack from the town on the Parliamentary trenches and several men were killed or wounded before the attackers were driven back by heavy musket-fire. That night Lord Grey's forces brought their guns close to Harrison's Barn, ready to open fire as soon as Essex gave the command.

But the siege was nearly over. Fielding had decided that his position was hopeless. The town was almost completely surrounded; neither the

65

promised ammunition nor the relief force had arrived, and it seemed more sensible to save his army than to let it be destroyed in the defence of the town. On Tuesday 25 April, at about 9 o'clock in the morning, he ordered the white flag to be hung out and sent a drummer to beat a parley.

Hostages, three officers from each side, had been exchanged, and terms of surrender were being discussed, when the Royalist forces arrived in strength on Caversham Heights, both the King and Prince Rupert being with them. Commanded by Rupert, and with Sir Lewis Dives' regiment in the van, the Cavaliers swept down the hillside and furiously assaulted the Parliamentary regiment guarding the bridge. A Royalist officer's account of that day describes how his troops had marched by wooded ways through Nettlebed to Caversham, and how between them and the bridge stood a great mud-walled barn, heavily fortified by the enemy; and how many gallant men were sent across an open field to storm the barn, and were picked off by enemy marksmen "like ripe fruit in a strong wind". A Parliamentary account claims that Royalists fell like leaves in autumn and that "it pleased the Lord in the midst of the fight to send amongst them a very violent and vehement shower of hail and rain", which the wind blew into the faces of the Cavaliers but only onto the backs of the Parliamentary soldiers.

The Royalists were utterly defeated, although somehow in the confusion they managed to get a supply of ammunition across the river into Reading. Late in the afternoon they retreated up the hillside, leaving many of their dead lying in the field, and several hundred wounded in barns and outhouses. The next morning Essex sent his own surgeons to attend to them, and ordered the local people to bury the dead where they lay.

Long after the fight had passed into history, and that open field in Caversham had become known as Balmore, a tradition lingered in the neighbourhood that there was once a day when Balmer's Field ran red with blood.

After the Siege

It was all in vain. Reading was surrendered. In spite of the fresh supply of ammunition and the advice of some of his officers Fielding would not forfeit his honour by breaking the truce. Prince Rupert was furious because the garrison had not come to his aid at Caversham, and it was only with severe displeasure that the King consented to the surrender of the town. Fielding was later court-martialled and never held command again.

On 27 April the Royalist garrison marched out of Reading and over Caversham Bridge, having been granted a free passage to Oxford. Sir Arthur Aston, in a horse litter covered with red cloth and lined with white, headed the column. He was soon to be appointed Governor of Oxford. Behind him followed coaches and wagons, and then the horse and foot regiments, marching with colours flying, drums beating and trumpets sounding, carrying their arms and ammunition with them. Under the terms of the treaty of capitulation they were allowed to take with them fifty carts to carry baggage and sick and wounded men. As the Royalists marched away to the north, Essex led his army into the town through the battered defences on the western side.

Although he had promised that the townspeople, no matter which side they supported, would not be subjected to ill-treatment or imprisonment and that their properties would not be plundered, Essex had great difficulty in controlling his men. As soon as they got inside the town some of them plundered the houses of the leading Royalists, and several ugly scenes took place before Essex, riding in person from street to street, succeeded in restoring order.

The Parliamentary army occupied Reading for about six weeks, as many as possible of the men being billeted in the town and the rest nearby. For Essex those were six weeks of continuous strain. Hundreds of his men were sick as a result of the unhealthy conditions in the riverside camps and in the overcrowded town. The 12 shillings he gave to every foot soldier for his service during the siege, and to discourage plundering, caused discontent among the horse regiments and among the officers. Six weeks of idleness allowed too much opportunity for heavy drinking in the taverns and alehouses, and led to further outbreaks of looting and violence. At the end of May he moved with part of his army to the higher ground of Caversham Park, where many of the sick recovered in the healthier environment. In July he marched away.

Reading remained in Parliamentary hands until the First Battle of Newbury had been fought on 20 September 1643, after which Essex withdrew his army to London. By the end of that month Reading had been reoccupied by Royalist forces, and a new Governor, Sir Jacob Astley, had been appointed. One of his first orders concerned the strengthening of the town's defences. Every householder was commanded to labour at repairing the bulwarks, or fined 12 pence for every day he failed to attend. The fines money was used to help pay poorer people 8 pence a day for doing the work. More taxes were levied to support the garrison and to provide an allowance of £7 a week for the Governor.

By the following Spring the war was going badly for the King, and Reading was under threat of another siege from Essex' army. In the middle of May 1644 Charles himself came to Reading, where he was entertained for a few days by Thomas Vachell at Coley Park. It was decided to make no attempt to hold the town. The King ordered the defences to be slighted and the town abandoned, "all such of his good subjects as were willing to be freed from the power of the Parliament's forces" being urged to follow him to Oxford.

By 20 May Essex was again in control of Reading. To his immediate demand for money the council replied that the King had graciously freed the town from the obligation to pay, and that they were utterly impoverished. Essex' next demand, that Caversham Bridge, broken by departing Royalists, should be repaired forthwith at the town's expense, met with a more cooperative response.

Having realised that possession of Reading gave them control of barge traffic on the Thames, Parliament took care to hold the town until the end of the war. Their garrison was at first too small, and in June 1644 Lieut. Colonel Lower, Deputy Governor of the Royalist garrison at Wallingford, took advantage of its weakness to kidnap the Mayor of Reading in order to extort money from the town.

Alderman William Brackston, who had reluctantly taken his oath as Mayor in the uncertain days after the Battle of Newbury, was now to have his reluctance fully justified. For three weeks Lower had been demanding a contribution of £50 a week towards the maintenance of the Wallingford garrison, and Reading had naturally refused to pay. On 22 June the town's senior Aldermen received a letter from the Mayor informing them that he had been carried away during the night by a party of horse, and would be detained as a prisoner at Wallingford until the contributions had been paid. Another letter from Lieut. Colonel Lower confirmed that the contributions amounted to £200.

The matter was "much debated and considered" by the Aldermen, who finally agreed that a submissive reply saying that they were willing but unable to pay should be sent, and that Councillor Samuel Johnson should ride to Wallingford to deliver this reply. After further negotiations, and an appeal for help to the King's Council of War at Oxford (Samuel Johnson was kept busy riding backwards and forwards) the demand was reduced to £100, and the Mayor was restored to his town in time to preside at a meeting on 10 July.

Soon after this incident a stronger garrison was sent to Reading and the town became the headquarters of the Parliamentary Committee for Berkshire, whose task was to administer local affairs and weed out Royalist sympathisers. Among its members were Daniel Blagrave of Southcote Lodge and Tanfield Vachell, whose house was in Friar Street. One of the Committee's first acts was to declare five members of the town council, including Anthony Brackston, clothier and uncle of the Mayor, and Thomas Harrison, brewer, to be persons notoriously disaffected to the State and unfit to remain in office. The council, however, took no action and most of the accused continued to attend meetings.

The Parliamentary Committee had, in any case, far more serious matters to attend to. The whole county was in a miserable condition. In the country districts "hardly a sheep, hen, hog, oats, hay, wheat or any other thing" was left for man or beast to feed on. Horses were in desperately short supply; the armies were now leaving worn out or wounded animals with the farmers and taking their work horses.

In Reading the long-suffering householders complained bitterly to Parliament that the soldiers broke into their houses, stole their goods, robbed their markets and threatened their magistrates; so that without speedy redress they would be constrained to abandon the town to the will of the soldiers, "who cry out they have no pay, they have no beds, they have no fire, and they must and will have it by force, or they will burn down all the houses in the town, whatever become of them."

In December 1644 Alderman Thomas Harrison asked to be removed from his place on the council on account of his increasing poverty, and at several subsequent meetings he demanded payment of the considerable sums of money he had loaned to the council early in the war. He was only one of many leading townsmen to whom the council was in debt. In March 1645 Daniel Blagrave, recently elected a member of the town council, discussed the matter with the Parliamentary Committee but, not surprisingly, the debts remained unpaid.

In July 1647 the King, now in the custody of the Parliamentary army, was lodged for a while at Caversham Park while the army council met in Reading to discuss their next move. Charles was allowed to ride under escort to Maidenhead where, at the Greyhound Inn, he was reunited with his younger children, the Princess Elizabeth and the Duke of Gloucester, who returned with him to spend two days at Caversham Park. Before the end of the month the army, together with its royal prisoner, had moved on towards London.

In January 1649 Daniel Blagrave, by that time representing Reading in Parliament, was one of the 59 Members who signed the death warrant of King Charles I. Parliament ruled the land for the next 11 years.

Religious Controversies

Although in 1660 the restoration of the monarchy was proclaimed in the Market Place "with great solemnity and rejoicing", and King Charles II's coronation in the following year was celebrated with freely flowing drink and merrily crackling bonfires, the more sober of Reading's citizens may well have viewed the future with foreboding.

While Parliament ruled, many of them had forsaken the ancient parish churches and banded together to form various Nonconformist congregations. The new King's crowning brought back official recognition of the Church of England. The royal arms, repainted, were once again displayed in the churches, and, a year later, Parliament passed the Act of Uniformity. This Act, together with other new legislation, placed severe restrictions upon everyone who refused to conform to the doctrines and worship of the Established Church. It was to lead to years of oppression and persecution.

Reading people, in particular, must have been bitterly reminded of the town's most distinguished son, William Laud, Archbishop of Canterbury, whose downfall the Puritans had brought about nearly twenty years before.

Born in Reading in 1573 and appointed Archbishop by Charles I in 1633, Laud had become one of the most powerful and most hated men in England. A fanatical high churchman, he had tried to impose his ideals of unity and order upon the Church throughout England, and even upon Presbyterian Scotland. Anyone who dared to oppose or criticise him too openly ran the risk of cruel punishment. A man named Ludovic Bowyer, who had rashly spread rumours in Reading that the Archbishop was in league with the Pope, was sentenced in London to hard labour for life, to have the letters L and R, for Liar and Rogue, burned on his forehead, and to stand in the pillory in London and in Reading Market Place with his ears nailed to the pillory and a paper on his head declaring the nature of his offence.

Such senseless cruelties could only increase Laud's unpopularity, and as the Puritan party gained strength so did effective opposition to Laud. When rebellion in Scotland, and a desperate need for money, compelled the King, after a break of eleven years, to summon Parliament, that body soon sent Laud to the Tower. He was brought to trial in 1643 and beheaded on Tower Hill on 10 January 1645.

Five years before his death a small community which he would have abominated began to meet in Reading. The Baptists had no regular ministry, no singing at their services, no church in which to worship. They survived the upheavals of the Civil War, and during Cromwell's Protectorate felt so secure that, in 1656, they began to keep records of their meetings. But after the Restoration the pages of their record book were left blank for many years. Their meetings had to be held in secret, informers guarded against, and a lookout kept if they were to avoid arrest and imprisonment. For several years they met in a house in Pinkneys Lane, backing onto the Holy Brook, across which they were able to throw a plank bridge and make their escape if the meeting was in danger of being interrupted. To the house in Pinkneys Lane the most famous of all Baptists, John Bunyan, came on more than one occasion to preach to them. He is said to have made his way through the town disguised as a wagoner in order to avoid recognition and arrest. Bunyan preached in Reading in August 1688, a few days before his death. A wet, cold ride back to London is believed to have brought on the fever of which he died.

The earliest meetings of the Quakers in Reading took place in the Spring of 1655, the first being held on the bowling green of the Broad Face Inn in Market Place. In July 1655 George Fox, founder of the Society of Friends, addressed a large crowd in an orchard on the south side of London Road, recording afterwards, "a glorious meeting it was and a great convincement of people there was that day."

After the Restoration the Quakers suffered more severe and continuous persecution than other Nonconformists. Their open defiance of the law and obstinate, passive resistance perplexed and infuriated the authorities. They did nothing secretly. Their meetings were held regularly in houses with open doors, so that all might enter, including informers, constables and magistrates, and the law might do as it pleased to try to break up the meetings.

In January 1662 all the Quakers at a meeting were thrown out of the house. At subsequent meetings names were taken and many were sent to prison. Others, including women and children, were roughly treated, and had bucketfuls of water thrown over them and their houses broken down. In July 1671 it was reported that there were 77 Quakers in Reading prison, and six others had died there. Of the 77 prisoners 28 men and 35 women were there for refusing to take the Oath of Allegiance to the King; others for non-payment of tithes, or of fines for not attending parish church services.

The Congregational Church in Reading owes its beginnings to a group of Independents who met at the house of the Rev Christopher Fowler after he had been ejected from his living at St Mary's, in 1662, on account of his Puritan proclivities and practices. Fowler's ministry did not last long, for he had many enemies among the Anglicans, one of whom called him "the author of most of the evil in the town." By the end of 1663 he was in prison and was never allowed to preach in Reading again. Some years later he was succeeded by the Rev Thomas Juice, during whose ministry Reading Congregationalists began to meet on the site in Broad Street where their present church stands.

The magistrates would have liked to put Mr Juice in prison, but he successfully evaded capture. For some time he was hidden, and supplied with food, by Mrs Thorne, wife of a tanner in Mill Lane. His place of concealment was the middle of a bark rick from which, when it was safe to do so, he crept out "to preach to his afflicted people."

The death of Charles II in 1685 brought to the throne his brother James, a Catholic who tried to rule with Catholic ministers. What the English people thought of this was made very clear by the Glorious Revolution of 1688, when James' Protestant son-in-law and daughter, William and Mary, were invited to occupy the throne instead of James.

William landed at Torbay early in November 1688 and advanced towards London, meeting with little resistance. James' army waited on Hounslow Heath to defend the capital, but an advance guard of several hundred horse and foot was sent to garrison Reading in order to intercept William as he approached along the highway from the west. So it came about that Reading was the only place at which blood was shed in the otherwise bloodless revolution.

Many of James' soldiers were Irish Catholics, hated and feared by most Englishmen at that time. In Reading fear bred panic, as a wild rumour spread that the soldiers intended to plunder the town and massacre the inhabitants while they were at their Sunday morning worship. Many terrified people fled. The soldiers posted sentries to stop anyone else leaving, and the panic grew worse. A messenger sent by the town council managed to evade the sentries and carry a plea for help to William, who had reached Hungerford. William despatched a relief force of about 350 Dutch troops, and learning of their approach the Reading garrison prepared for battle. As the Dutch were expected to enter the town along the Bath Road, a body of horse was posted at the bottom of Castle Street, and the walls of St Mary's churchyard were lined with musketeers. Other troops were drawn up in Broad Street, while the main body stood ready in the Market Place. On the tower of St Mary's Church a lookout was posted with orders to fire his musket and ring the bell as soon as he caught sight of the Dutch.

The townspeople, having watched these preparations, contrived to send another messenger to warn the Dutch, with the result that the advancing troops cut across the fields from the Bath Road to the lane coming from Pangbourne and, hidden by tall hedges, made their way into the town before the lookout spotted them. The Irish were caught completely off their guard. One body of Dutch stormed down the Butts and attacked them in Castle Street and in the churchyard; another fell upon the troops in Broad Street. The Irish were over-whelmed and retreated in such disorder down Minster Street, Broad Street and London Street that the troops waiting in the Market Place mistook the situation and fled in confusion. They were all chased out of Reading as far as Twyford, their departure being hastened by jubilant townspeople, who fired on them from the windows of their houses. The Irish lost about 50 men, the Dutch half-a-dozen. Some of the dead were buried in St Giles' churchyard.

The Reading Fight of 9 December 1688 was celebrated for more than a century afterwards. On the anniversary church bells rang a peal of triumph, and the fight was remembered by the singing of a ballad, to the tune of Lillibulero:

> Five hundred Papishes came there
> To make a final end
> Of all the town, in time of prayer,
> But God did them defend . . .

William and Mary were crowned in 1689, and in the same year the Toleration Act granted freedom of worship to Protestant Nonconformists.

Eighteenth Century Enterprises – Travel and Transport

In contrast to the political and religious strife and economic uncertainty of the 17th century, the 18th century brought a long period of domestic peace and steady economic growth. Expanding commercial interests demanded and achieved, although slowly, improved communications by road and water. Experiments in agricultural methods and husbandry produced better crops and fatter animals. Prosperity encouraged the building of brick and stone houses in the new symmetrical style of architecture, replacing the old timber-framed structures. The growing demand for fine furniture, porcelain and other domestic luxuries enabled craftsmanship to flourish. Towards the end of the century civic pride began to find expression in new public buildings and street improvements.

At the beginning of the century Reading was a fairly prosperous if rather shabby country town. "Its houses", wrote Thomas Hearne, the Berkshire-born antiquary, "are very mean and the streets, though pretty large, unpaved." The town's economy had been slow to recover from the dire effects of the Civil War, and its poverty was prolonged because no successful new industries had been established to replace the moribund clothing trade. Reading's livelihood had come to depend largely upon its continuing importance as the marketing centre for the produce of the surrounding countryside; its corn market was soon to be regarded as one of the best in England. But its geographical situation astride the great western highway and beside the Thames waterway ensured that Reading revived to enjoy a new age of commercial prosperity.

People and events outside Reading, and the ways of the world of fashion, were to play their part in the process of revival. Queen Anne, whose short reign ushered in the 18th century, was for much of her life an invalid. Gout and dropsy, combined with a liking for a quiet life, drove her from the noise, bustle and smoke of London into the country, where Windsor Castle was one of her favourite residences. In

London Road, part of the great road from London to Bath which became famous in the 18th century, from a print published in 1823.

the summer of 1702 her search for better health led her to try the waters at Bath. The place, as well as the waters, suited her so well that she became a regular visitor, and, where the Queen went, society was bound to follow. Soon crowds of people were flocking to Bath, which became one of the most beautiful and civilised towns in England. Its popularity as a summer resort for English society long outlived the reign of Anne and lasted throughout the 18th century.

As a result the main highway from London to the west country was transformed into the famous and fashionable Bath Road of the coaching era. Towns and villages all along its route benefited from increased traffic. In those days travel, even for rich people, was slow. The roughness of the road surface, the jolting discomfort of the heavy carriages, the need to rest and change horses every eight or ten miles, made numerous stopping places essential. The wealthy travellers, whose numbers were increasing, demanded better food, accommodation and attention for themselves and their horses and carriages than had formerly been available at many places along the road. Innkeepers strove to please, prospered, took on more servants and enlarged their premises. In places such as Slough, Twyford, Theale, Woolhampton, Speenhamland and Hungerford, inns were among the most prominent buildings; centres of activity and excitement as the coaches and carriages arrived and departed. The innkeepers' prosperity was shared by local shopkeepers, farriers, wheelwrights and other tradesmen, all of whom profited from new business.

In Reading, old-established inns, such as the Crown in Crown Street and the Bear in Bridge Street, both on the principal route through the town, became the favoured hostelries of the nobility and gentry. Both inns were enlarged and refurbished during the 18th century. Other flourishing inns were the George, the Ship and the Sun, all still in existence, the Broad Face and the Saracen's Head on the eastern side of the Market Place, the Angel in Broad Street, which became one of the busiest coach stations when regular public coach services began to run in the 1780s, and the King's Arms which enjoyed a salubrious situation as well as a fine view at the top of Castle Hill where the Bath Road enters Reading. There were many more.

While the nobility and gentry in their pursuit of pleasure were making their way along the Bath Road between Reading and Newbury, the River Kennet in the valley to the south was undergoing changes in the interests of trade and commerce. For centuries heavy and bulky goods, which pack horses and wagons could not carry along the roads, had been carried by water. Their journeys along winding rivers were slow and often dangerous. Natural hazards were provided by shallows, rapids and floods, and artificial hazards by millers, each of whom needed to build a dam to provide a head of water to drive his mill. By the 17th century waterborne trade had increased so greatly that improvements to river navigation were very necessary, and extensions to the inland waterways system highly desirable. In particular, the immense benefits which could result from linking the two ports of London and Bristol via the Avon and the Thames inspired many ambitious schemes, but it was not until the early years of the 19th century that this dream was to become a reality.

In 1708 a more modest scheme was put forward to make navigable the River Kennet from Newbury to Reading, thus enabling Newbury to develop as a distribution centre for a wide area in west Berkshire and neighbouring Wiltshire. Towns and villages to the west of Newbury supported the scheme; Reading opposed it, fearing that it would lose its supremacy as the distribution centre for the county. Shopkeepers and innkeepers protested that they would lose custom if fewer people came to buy and sell in Reading. The town council gloomily envisaged a falling-off from tolls if business at the wharves declined.

Their opposition, which was fierce and prolonged, succeeded only in delaying the project. The Kennet Navigation Act was passed in Parliament in 1715 and work commenced. During the first three years little progress was made, the planners inevitably having little previous knowledge of such an enterprise, but in 1718 a new engineer and surveyor, John Hore of Newbury, was appointed and instructed to make a new survey. The plan Hore prepared reduced the meandering course of the Kennet between Newbury and Reading to a distance of only 18$\frac{1}{2}$ miles, making cuts for 11$\frac{1}{2}$ miles and following the natural course of the stream for 7 miles. The rise of 134 feet in level from Reading was overcome by the construction of 20 locks. His plan was approved.

Work on the canal was making good progress and had reached Burghfield when, in 1720, the smouldering hostility of Reading's inhabitants flared into violence. A mob, about 300 strong and including the Recorder and the Mayor (Robert Blake, whose wharf lay on the north bank of the Kennet beyond Blake's Bridge), marched out across the fields and deliberately destroyed part of the canal works. The canal proprietors threatened prosecution. The Mayor and the Recorder, in a more sober frame of mind, undertook to keep the peace in future and to use their influence to prevent any further outbreaks of violence.

The Kennet Navigation was opened to traffic in 1723 and in the following year the remaining work which needed to be done on the horse towing path was completed. Trade immediately began to build up, with barges carrying loads of meal, flour, cheese and other agricultural produce to London and returning with loads of coal, iron, groceries and other heavy goods.

Passing through Reading must, however, have been an ordeal for bargemen using the new navigation. In spite of the promises of the Mayor and the Recorder, Reading people continued to express their hostility to the enterprise in words and deeds of violence. In July 1725 a notable anonymous letter was sent to Peter Darvall, a Maidenhead bargemaster who worked a boat along the Kennet. It was dated from Reading on 10 July and said:

"Mr Darvall, wee bargemen of Redding thought to Aquaint you before 'tis too Late, Dam You, if y. work a bote any more to Newbery wee will Kill You if ever you come any more this way, we was very near shooting you last time, wee went with to pistolls and was not too Minnets too Late. The first time your Boat Lays at Redding Loaded, Dam You, wee will bore hols in her and sink her so Dont come to starve our fammeleys and our Masters, for Dam You if you do wee will send you short home . . ."

There is no record of Mr Darvall, or his boat, having suffered the threatened fate.

At Theale, overt obstructive action was taken by Simon Finch, the miller at Sheffield Mill, then the property of the Borough of Reading. Finch diverted all the water in the pound through his mill gates, effectively preventing the passage of barges through the lock. One bargeman had to unload most of his 50 tons of cargo in order to pass through and when, having reloaded, he reached Reading he was pelted with stones by people lining the banks. Another bargeman, carrying 30 chaldrons of coal from London to Newbury, was held up for eight days at Sheffield Mill and eventually turned round and went back to Reading. Simon Finch's action involved the town council in a long and troublesome dispute with the Kennet Navigation proprietors, the costs to the council amounting to more than £250.

A few years later, when it had become obvious that the new canal was in no way detrimental to the commercial interests of Reading, the townspeople grew more tolerant. As well they might. In the 1740s their town was said to be "very large and wealthy", and they themselves "rich, and driving a very great trade." *A Tour through the Island of Great Britain,* published about 1748, said of Reading, "the town is situated on the River Kennet, but so near the Thames, that the largest barges which they use may come up to the Town Bridge, where they have wharfs to load and unload them. Their chief trade is by this water-navigation to and from London, tho' they have necessarily a great trade into the country, for the consumption of the goods which they bring by their barges from London; and, particularly, coals, salt, grocery-wares, tobacco, oils, and all heavy goods."

So the Kennet bargemen were allowed to work in peace, and the town of Newbury was able to build up a similar trade to that of Reading. In the 1760s the navigation company carried out a number of profitable improvements, among which was the acquisition of additional facilities by renting Blake's Wharf in Reading for £150 a year.

By the 1780s schemes to link the Kennet and the Avon were under serious consideration and, in 1794, the Kennet & Avon Canal Act was passed. In December 1810 the long-desired link creating a continuous waterway between London and Bristol was completed.

Eighteenth Century Enterprises – The Reading Mercury

The summer of 1723 saw the birth of another far-reaching enterprise when the first issue of the *Reading Mercury* appeared on Monday 8 July. The *Mercury* was the brainchild of William Parks and David Kinnier, two printers who had recently set up in business next door to the ancient Saracen's Head Inn in High Street (demolished in the 19th century when King's Road was built). At their shop, they claimed, "all manner of Printing Business is handsomely done, as Books, Advertisements, Summons, Subpoenas, Funeral-Tickets, &c. Shop keepers Bills are done here after the best manner, with the Prints of their Signs, or other proper Ornaments. Also Gentlemen may have their Coats of Arms, or other Fancies curiously cut in Wood, or engrav'd in Mettal."

In the first issue of the *Mercury* Messrs Parks and Kinnier expressed their surprise that the art of printing had not previously been established in Reading, when presses had already been set up in several smaller towns. "We have, however, pitched our tent here, induced by the good character this country bears, for pleasure and plenty, and intend, with your leave, to publish a weekly newspaper, under the title of The Reading Mercury, or Weekly Entertainer."

A flattering portrait followed of the county and town of their choice. In Berkshire, "the air is sweet; the soil plentiful; the whole county is well stored with corn, cattle, fish, fowl, wool and wood, especially oak." Of Reading they said, "The market, which is reputed one of the best in England for all sorts of grain and other provisions, is on Saturdays . . . The meadows within the limits of the said Borough, if equalled, are not exceeded by any in England, for pleasure and fertility, especially that called the King's Mead, which joins to the River Thames. It hath 4 fairs a year; hath been very famous for the clothing trade, but now is so for malt-making. 'Tis well served with river water, laid into the houses of the inhabitants; it hath a very good free grammar school, to which belongs two Fellowships at St John's

College at Oxford; and two other charity schools; one being now rebuilding in a handsome manner; and several almshouses for poor men and women."

Before 1723 people in the Reading area who had wanted to read newspapers had arranged to have them sent by post from London, a fairly costly business. Now they were able to keep in touch with news of the Royal Family, political events, the world of commerce, and the shocking misdeeds of highwaymen and other criminals through the columns of their own newspaper, most of which consisted of extracts from the London newspapers. Local news was not, at first, considered of sufficient interest to print, most of the towns and villages served by the paper being small enough for all their news to be spread by word of mouth. The only local news story in the first issue of the *Mercury* was a bald account of the accidental death of a Reading man: "Last Wednesday a person of this town riding in his cart to fetch hay, and whipping the horses too fast, they ran against a hedge and overturned the cart, by which fall he was so mortally bruised, that he died in less than an hour after." Not until the second half of the 18th century was local news allotted a regular space, and full-time reporting of local affairs was not introduced until the 19th century.

In its early years the circulation of the *Mercury* was small, only about 400 copies being printed each week, and those mainly for regular subscribers. Few copies were available for casual sales at the printing office. The paper was delivered by newsmen to the town or country homes of the subscribers, where its arrival was welcomed by the household as one of the more exciting events of the week.

The newsmen, some of whom became well-known characters, covered the same routes through outlying villages and hamlets throughout the year, travelling mostly on foot, but sometimes on horseback or with a horse and cart. Only rarely was delivery of the paper delayed by bad weather, even in the severest winters. In remote rural areas the newsmen were doubly welcome, because, like the pedlars of an earlier age, they carried with them an assortment of commodities, such as patent medicines, pins, cottons and also books, pamphlets and ballads printed at the *Mercury* office.

As the area of circulation of the *Mercury* grew and became too large for the newsmen to cover directly from Reading, agents were set up in nearby towns, such as Wokingham, to help distribute supplies. Towards the end of the century a wider readership was made possible by the introduction of the regular mail coach services. In 1784 the inauguration of the mail coach service along the Bath Road from London to Bristol was soon taken advantage of by the proprietors of the *Mercury,* who informed their readers that, "The Mail leaving this town at a very early hour ... the printers will now be under the necessity of putting this paper to press much earlier than usual, that they may not lose the advantage of this regular conveyance ..." As a result of their enterprise copies of the *Mercury* were available as far away as Marlborough by eight o'clock in the morning.

The proprietorship of the *Mercury* changed several times in the first few years, neither Parks nor Kinnier remaining long in Reading. In 1737 the paper was bequeathed by William Carnan to his brother Charles and to John Newbery, a young man who had joined the firm seven years earlier. Newbery, however, was ambitious and more interested in bookselling than in running a provincial newspaper. While retaining his part-ownership of the *Mercury* for some years, he moved to London, where he set up a bookshop and won lasting fame as the first publisher of children's books. He died in 1767 and was buried at Waltham St Lawrence, where he had been born.

In 1762 the proprietorship passed to Anna Maria, daughter of William Carnan and wife of the poet Christopher Smart. Her marriage had taken place secretly ten years before, and, upon its becoming known, her husband had been compelled to give up his Fellowship of Pembroke Hall, Cambridge. Christopher Smart moved to London where he earned a precarious living as a poet, contributing to various literary and satirical journals. He was befriended and aided by Dr Johnson and David Garrick, as well as by John Newbery and the Carnan family, but his life was ruined by increasingly severe bouts of insanity. His illness separated him from his wife and daughters, and most of his later years were spent in a madhouse, where, nevertheless, he wrote his finest poem *The Song to David.* He died in 1771 at the age of 49.

After the break-up of her unfortunate marriage Anna Maria built up a new life as a business-woman. For over forty years she ran the *Reading Mercury,* at first in partnership with her brother, John Carnan, who dealt with the printing side of the business, and, after his death in 1785, with Thomas Cowslade. The latter had married her elder daughter, Marianne, and it was to the Cowslades that the *Mercury* passed when Mrs Smart died in 1809. They were to own it until the beginning of the 20th century.

Eighteenth Century Enterprises: Industries and Improvements

The modern prosperity of Reading was founded in the 18th century when the town began to develop a variety of industries, rather than one major industry. At the same time its advantageous position as a centre of communications began to be more profitably exploited.

At The Oracle, by then a century old but partly restored during the mayoralty of John Watts in the 1720s for the better accommodation of the poor, pinmaking and silk weaving were carried on. Pins had been made in Reading since the reign of Elizabeth and their manufacture was to remain a thriving industry until it was killed by the rivalry of Birmingham in the 19th century. Silk weaving, begun in the 17th century, was carried on in various parts of the town, ribbons and satins also being made, but this industry died out about the middle of the 19th century. At The Oracle, and at Katesgrove, sailcloth was made, and was heavily in demand for the ships of the East India Company and for those of the Royal Navy during the Napoleonic wars. Reading sailcloth helped to win the Battle of Trafalgar.

Brickmaking had long been established as a local industry, particularly in the Tilehurst area, and kilns were also working in Katesgrove by the end of the 18th century. One of Reading's earliest iron-foundries (another industry which developed in Katesgrove in the 19th century) was started by Benjamin Williams in 1790. About this time an appetising aroma was introduced into the town's industrial atmosphere when James Cocks began to make Cocks' Reading Sauce, destined to reign as a household favourite in England and overseas for more than a century.

Throughout the 18th century the wharves along the Kennet were the scene of constant activity, and an increasing variety of goods could be seen being loaded and unloaded. On some of the wharves huge quantities of timber from the thickly wooded parts of the county were stacked waiting to be sent to London, where it was used, among other purposes, for building merchant ships. But the principal cargo was malt made from the abundant crops of barley which were grown all over Berkshire. By the middle of the century some of the barges carrying malt were said to be so large that they contained between 100 and 120 tons. In the 18th century more use began to be made of the local supply of malt when beer brewing became a major industry in all the chief towns, and many villages, in Berkshire.

For hundreds of years ale had been part of the staple diet of the population, and had been brewed in Reading as in other towns. In the 16th century, when hops had been introduced into England long enough to be widely cultivated, beer brewers began to set up in business everywhere. By the 17th century there were several flourishing brewers in Reading, memorably Alderman Thomas Harrison of Civil War fame. In London, Puritans protested that "this wicked weed (the hop plant) would spoil the drink and endanger the lives of the people", but their protests were of no avail. Beer drinking had come to stay.

John Watts, Reading's enterprising mayor, tried to establish a Hop Fair, to be held annually on the same day as the great Cheese Fair (21 September). An advertisement was accordingly placed in the London newspapers as well as in the *Reading Mercury* for three successive years, 1724-7, but the proposal did not then arouse sufficient interest. Mr Watts' idea was ahead of his time; he would have been pleased to know that a Hop Fair was in fact held in Reading in the middle of the 19th century.

Reading's most famous brewery was founded in Broad Street in 1785 by William Blackall Simonds. The site soon proved too small and in 1790 he moved to a larger one in Bridge Street beside the Kennet. Seven Bridges House was designed for him by Sir John Soane in 1790, and built to house the Simonds family beside their brewery. Although there were four other breweries in Reading at the time, notably Stephens' Brewery, which was producing 25,000 barrels of beer and porter annually, Simonds' continued to prosper. In the 19th century it became the largest in Reading, owning numerous public houses in the surrounding countryside and enjoying a highly profitable trade with the Army, both at home and overseas.

During the 18th century Reading began to reflect its new-found prosperity in the appearance of its streets and buildings. The process of renewal was slow to begin with, but accelerated in the last quarter of the century.

The 1720s saw the rebuilding of the Blue Coat Schol, which had been founded and endowed for 20 boys by Richard Aldworth in 1646 and opened ten years later. Subsequent benefactors had increased the number of places for scholars to 36, so that the original building was badly overcrowded as well as in a serious state of disrepair. It was rebuilt on the same site at the corner of Silver Street and London Road.

About the same time the road leading from Reading to Caversham, then graphically named Caversham Water or Watery Lane, underwent some long overdue repairs. The expenses were defrayed by public subscription, as Lord Cadogan, then owner of Caversham Park and High Steward of Reading had failed to carry out his promise to have the work done at his own expense.

In 1760 King Street was formed by the demolition of a row of old houses running down the centre of it and dividing it into two narrow lanes called Sun Lane and Back Lane. The new wide street so created was named King Street to mark the accession that year of George III. A similar row of medieval buildings dividing the eastern end of Broad Street into Fisher Row and Butcher Row remained standing until the following century.

In the 1780s municipal enterprise achieved further improvements to the centre of the town, although some of them met with strong opposition. Some improvement to the streets was certainly necessary, their uneven flint and pebble surfaces and water-filled hollows having long been the cause of complaints from residents as well as from visitors to the town. The condition of the streets was the result of years of haphazard repair and maintenance, it having long been the custom for each householder to repair the road in front of his premises. In addition there were numerous obstructions, such as rails, posts, protruding bay windows and trees, which made the passage of pedestrians and traffic more difficult and dangerous, particularly at night.

Picturesque though the streets may have been, and redolent of their historic past, the council decided that changes must be made. In 1785, during the mayoralty of John Deane, application was made to Parliament for an act authorising the council to pave the footways, provide for the better cleansing, lighting and watching of the streets, and to levy the necessary rate to pay for these improvements.

For several weeks the townspeople, almost equally divided on the issue, were engaged in heated controversy. Those in favour felt that they had suffered long enough from the existing state of affairs and that it was time the street surfaces matched up to the smart new houses

Simonds' Brewery steam lorry and trailer, 1924.

which were beginning to replace the old lath and plaster ones. The businessmen among them predicted that the improvements would attract wealthy new residents to the area and help to invigorate trade. Those against the measure objected mainly on the grounds of expense, but some feared that a wholesale destruction of houses might ensue for the purpose of widening streets and erecting new buildings.

In March the Reading Paving Bill was read for the first time in the House of Commons, and a petition from those against it was also presented. At the second reading in May one of Reading's Members of Parliament, Francis Annesley, opposed it, claiming that it was not supported by the majority of the inhabitants. The other, Richard Aldworth Neville, said cautiously that he believed that the inhabitants were nearly equally divided on the matter and proposed that it should be referred to a committee for further discussion. This was done, and the Reading Paving Act was passed on 20 June 1785. A month later the *Mercury* announced that a public subscription had been opened for the more speedy accomplishment of the street paving, and published a list of the names of those who had already generously subscribed. Several members of the Mayor's family, Mr R.A. Neville, M.P., and Mrs Anna Maria Smart were among them.

On 8 August the ceremony of laying the first paving stone took place, the Paving Commissioners appointed to carry out the Act having all agreed that the first stone should lie before the door of the Mayor's house in Castle Street, in recognition of his initiative and attention to the improvement of the town. It was a day of celebration. A crowd of friends and supporters gathered at the Ship Inn at 10 o'clock in the morning and marched from there to the Mayor's house. A band played, church bells rang and flags fluttered along the streets. After the stone-laying ceremony the Mayor entertained his guests with an elegant and plentiful cold collation. Later in the day the gentlemen returned to the Ship for a splendid dinner in the Mayor's honour, and as night fell the festivities were completed with a display of fireworks.

The paving work being in progress, the council members turned their attention to the hall in which they met to deliberate on the town's affairs and receive the public at various functions. This was still the same hall, on the upper floor of the former abbey hospitium building, which they had begun to use over 200 years earlier. It was now showing the weight of its years in structural weaknesses, and, although impressive and historic, was unsuitable for its present purpose. A row of massive stone pillars supporting the pointed arches overhead extended down the length of the room, dividing it into two and making it inconvenient for large gatherings. A recent meeting of the Berkshire freeholders to nominate candidates for Parliament had had to be moved out to the Forbury because the hall was too small to hold more than a quarter of those attending. At assembly balls and concerts the pillars were a serious obstruction to dancers and audiences.

In 1785-6 the old hall was taken down and replaced by a new one built to the designs of Alderman Charles Poulton, by trade a cabinet maker. It comprised a spacious assembly room, whose walls and ceiling were decorated in the prevailing style of classical elegance, and an adjoining council chamber, on the walls of which were hung portraits of former benefactors of the borough, including Archbishop Laud, Sir Thomas White, Richard Aldworth and John Kendrick. The opening of the new Town Hall in August 1786 was marked by a concert of vocal and instrumental works by Handel and Haydn, followed by a grand ball.

In February 1787 the ruinous state of High Bridge at the bottom of

London Street was under discussion in the council chamber, and it was agreed that the sum of £3,500 should be spent on a new stone bridge, to be built in a handsome and substantial manner. The old timber bridge was, for the time being, to be made safe enough for the passage of horsemen and light carriages, but no heavy wagons were to be allowed over it.

The new bridge was designed by a London architect, Robert Brettingham. When it was opened at the end of November 1787 the first person to cross it was Mr Knight of Whitley, a very elderly gentleman whose life spanned almost the whole of the 18th century. He could remember, he said, riding behind his father across the former wooden bridge when it had just been built, and that was in 1707.

While the new Town Hall and High Bridge were being satisfactorily completed the paving Commissioners had been making slow progress with their task, and it was not until 1791 that the paving of some of the principal streets was completed. "This improvement", commented *The Universal Directory,* published in 1796, "added to the salubrity of the air and pleasantness of situation, renders this borough a pleasing place of retirement; and from the numerous respectable families who have recently made it their residence, it may truly be said to be considerably increased in rank, fashion and respectability, and now only needs the general additional ornament of lamps . . ."

Lamps were certainly needed. The town possessed only three street lamps, the lighting elsewhere being — as the repair of the streets had formerly been — the responsibility of the householders, who were supposed to place lanterns or candles outside their houses. The Paving Commissioners set to work again and, by 1801, the main streets were illuminated during the dark nights of winter by 174 oil lamps bracketed to the walls of houses.

Reading at the end of the Eighteenth Century

Reading was now a place of many attractions. It was not only a thriving commercial centre but a pleasant residential town, offering a variety of social amenities, several churches and chapels, and a number of schools, some of which provided, according to the lights of the time, a good education.

Like many other towns, it was a place of strong contrasts. Wide and dignified thoroughfares, such as Castle Street and London Street, were lined with well-built houses and presented pleasing prospects as they curved gracefully down into the town. The Market Place, paved and kept neat and clean, was surrounded by tastefully decorated shops where, it was said, goods of every description could be obtained as cheaply as in London. But behind most street frontages in the older parts of the town lay a network of narrow courts and alleyways, where tiny cottages crowded around dingy, sunless yards; and in the less fashionable shopping areas traders' stalls stood among heaps of rotting refuse, and open slaughterhouses offered passers-by a full view of live animals being butchered.

Street cleaning in most parts of the town was minimal, even some of the best houses having a heap of rubbish and manure in the gutter outside their front doors. But these were things which had long been taken for granted, and it was not until well into the next century that street cleaning became a matter of public concern.

Greater freedom of religious worship had allowed the numbers of churches and chapels to increase. Among the dissenters, the Baptists met in Hosiers Lane, the Quakers in Church Lane and the Congregationalists in Broad Street.

Catholics were able to hear mass in a tenement in Finch's Buildings, in Hosiers Lane. They owed this facility to Mrs Anna Maria Smart, who had raised the money to buy the tenement in order to provide a refuge for some of the hundreds of émigré priests then fleeing from the Revolution in France. About 1796 the King's Arms Inn, at the top of

Castle Hill, was requisitioned by the British Government to accommodate over 200 of these exiles. Mass was celebrated there daily in a large room formerly used for social gatherings at the inn. In 1812 the first Catholic church in Reading was built in Vastern Lane (now Blagrave Street), near Reading School. From 1802 another Catholic community worshipped in a chapel built by James Wheble at Woodley Lodge. Wheble also gave the site in Reading for St James' Catholic Church, opened in 1840.

In 1798 an evangelical chapel was built at the bottom of Castle Street on the site of the old county gaol, which was demolished when a new prison was built in Forbury Road. The chapel owed its foundation to the secession of part of the congregation of St. Giles', who objected to the vicar appointed to succeed the scholarly and well-loved William Bromley Cadogan. The chapel was built to seat 1,000, and it was so popular that it was usually full. Its most effective and influential minister was the Reverend James Sherman (1821-36) whose great gifts as a preacher drew such large crowds that the congregation often overflowed into the street. In 1840 the severely plain front of the building was enhanced by the addition of Corinthian columns and a square tower, which have since made the church a notable architectural feature at the foot of Castle Street.

Reading School at that time was enjoying the most famous period of its history. After the rebuilding of the Town Hall in 1786 a new school was built beside it by Dr Richard Valpy, who had been appointed headmaster in 1781. Dr Valpy was a distinguished classical scholar and author of several educational books, including a Latin grammar. The strictness of his discipline earned him the nickname of 'the mighty flogger', but the high standard of education provided during the 49 years of his headmastership won for the school an excellent reputation. By the time he retired in 1830 he had increased the number of pupils at the school to 120. Many of them were boarders, the sons of noblemen and gentlemen from all over England.

Across the Forbury, then a rough open space used as a playground by the boys of Reading School, stood the remains of the inner gateway of the Abbey. Here, for an unknown number of years up to 1796, was the Abbey School for girls, where the daughters of the gentry enjoyed a far more easy-going course of education than that provided at Dr Valpy's school. The Abbey's most famous pupil — although she did not remain there long and the exact dates of her attendance are unknown — was Jane Austen, who was sent there with her sister

The inner gateway of Reading Abbey at the end of the 18th century. The new brick building to the left housed the Abbey School, where Jane Austen was a pupil.

Cassandra in the early 1780s.

The school occupied rooms over the gateway and in a brick house adjoining it on the eastern side. In front of this house was a walled, tree-shaded garden where the girls were allowed to spend a great deal of time lazing and gossiping. From 1791-3 the Abbey School was attended by Martha Mary Butt, born in the same year as Jane Austen and destined to make her name in the literary world as Mrs Sherwood, author of a popular tale for children entitled *The Fairchild Family,* first published in 1817. Fortunately, Mrs Sherwood left a record of her schooldays.

She wrote in her memoirs that the school was run by a Mrs Latournelle and a Mme St Quintin, both English by birth. Mrs Latournelle was a middle-aged motherly lady, remarkable for having a cork leg, who saw to the domestic comforts of the establishment and left the teaching to her colleague. Mme St Quintin had taught at the school for some years and had married one of the many Frenchmen who fled to England from the Revolution. Her husband was befriended by Dr Valpy, who engaged him as a French teacher at Reading School. M. St. Quintin also acted as a tutor in French to the girls at the Abbey School. Another of his friends in Reading was Dr George Mitford. Some years after the Abbey School was closed and the St Quintins had opened another school in London, one of their pupils was Mary Russell Mitford, who was to become famous as the author of *Our Village,* a series of essays and stories about Three Mile Cross.

In addition to the many private academies for young ladies or gentlemen which then existed in the town, there was at least one school which provided for some of the hundreds of poor girls who would one day have to earn their livings. The Green School, so named from the colour of the girls' dresses, was founded in 1782 by a body composed of senior aldermen and the three parish vicars. It was a boarding school where girls were "trained up in the principles of the christian religion, in virtue and modesty, in honesty and truth, in decency, humility, civility and in mutual kindness, and in all due subordination." They were also taught reading, writing and arithmetic, and eventually sent out into the world as apprentices or domestic servants. The Green School was founded in St Mary's Butts and, in 1790, was moved to a substantial building on the north side of Broad Street, where it remained until the 1880s. It ended its days in Russell Street.

The social amenities of the town, particularly its entertainments, were well patronised by the nobility and gentry of the neighbourhood. As well as the regular assemblies and concerts they were able to enjoy meetings at Reading Races, held for many years on Bulmershe Heath, and performances during the summer season at the Reading Theatre, built in Friar Street in 1788 by actor-manager Henry Thornton. The larger inns accommodated social gatherings for dancing and card playing, and many political meetings, the Bear being the meeting place of the Tories and the Crown that of the Whigs.

At the end of the 18th century Reading was surrounded by country houses, some very old, some comparatively new, some still belonging to families who had lived in them for hundreds of years, some having passed through the hands of many owners, or having been recently purchased by newly-rich but unlanded gentlemen anxious to acquire a country property.

On the western side of the town the old moated manor house at Southcote was still occupied by the Blagraves, who had acquired it in the 16th century; but the neighbouring Coley estate, which had belonged to the Vachell family from the 14th century, had passed into new ownership in 1727.

Coley had, for many years, presented an impressive sight to the visitor approaching it down the tree-lined avenue. The last Tanfield Vachell to live there had, towards the end of the 17th century, caused the house to be rebuilt and the gardens laid out in a geometrical arrangement of paths and flower beds according to the Dutch-influenced fashion of that time. It was, perhaps, not surprising that the estate was heavily encumbered when he died in 1705. Sometime in the 18th century his house and gardens were swept away and a new house was built on higher ground away from the Holy Brook. This may have been done for William Chamberlayne, Esq., who purchased Coley in 1792. Today, only the old dovecote and farm buildings remain near the original site of Coley House.

At Calcot a large and well-timbered park on the sheltered southern side of Tilehurst, overlooking the Bath Road, surrounded Calcot House, a fine brick mansion built in 1755 for one of the many

Calcot Park House, built for John Blagrave in 1755.

Blagraves whose christian name was John. House and park have been the home of Calcot Golf Club since 1929.

A neighbouring estate at Prospect Hill had once been a farm belonging to the Kendrick family. In 1759 a small house was built in the woods there by Benjamin Child, widower of the Frances Kendrick whose highly original method of getting a husband by challenging him either to fight a duel with her or marry her inspired the popular ballad *The Berkshire Lady*. After Child's death the house was occupied by his daughter and her husband, but about 1800 it was purchased and enlarged by John Engelbert Liebenrood, whose colonnaded mansion, although sadly derelict, is still the focal point of Prospect Park.

On the Oxfordshire side of the Thames, Mapledurham House, hidden away between woods and river, was still the home of the Blounts, who entertained Sir Arthur Aston during the Civil War and, in the early years of the 18th century, the poet Alexander Pope.

At Caversham, prominently situated on the hillside stood Caversham park. This was no longer the house which had belonged to the Earl of Craven and where Charles I had stayed, but an elegant mansion in the classical style, built by Lord Cadogan in 1723. Its magnificence was enhanced by a terrace, said to be 1800 feet in length, overlooking extensive formal gardens embellished with statues, lakes, and avenues of trees.

A later owner of Caversham park was Major Charles Marsack, who purchased it in 1783 and spent lavishly to make house and grounds even more magnificent than before. Marsack, who had recently retired from the Indian Army, was rumoured to be an illegitimate son of George II. Like many rich men who had lived in India his ostentatious style of living and rather overbearing manner made him unwelcome in the best English society. Among local people, he made himself unpopular by not allowing them to pass freely through his park, as Lord Cadogan had done. The strange retinue he brought with him, said to include "old French women, Swiss valets, Gentoo coachmen, Mulatto footmen, and Negro butlers", also provoked a good deal of satirical gossip.

Martha Sherwood, in her schooldays at the Abbey in the 1790s, was taken by Mrs Valpy to visit Caversham Park. "There was much, when I visited the house," she wrote, "to bring India before me, amongst other things a splendid tapestry representing a royal cavalcade on a march, with camels and elephants. We were taken, before dinner, to a hot-house, where the Major presented me with a capsicum, telling me it was

Caversham Park, from a print published in 1793 during the ownership of Major Marsack. Marsack caused some fine beech trees in the park to be cut down, thus earning himself the nickname of Mr Massacre.

some sort of fine fruit, laughing heartily when I put some of it in my mouth. He had a delicate young wife, and several little children, but I did not envy her with all her splendour."

Major Marsack was one of several Nabobs who returned from India and purchased estates near Reading. Others were Francis Sykes at Basildon, George Vansittart at Bisham Abbey, William Watts at South Hill Park, Edward Golding at Maiden Erlegh, and William Byam Martin at Whiteknights. Edward Golding, whose fortune had been made with the East India Company, returned to England in 1780 and invested a great deal of his money in landed property in Berkshire. He pursued a political career, becoming an M.P. and a Lord of the Treasury. He carried out many improvements at Maiden Erlegh, which was to remain in his family until 1878.

The estate of Earley Whiteknights, formed before the Norman Conquest, had passed to the Englefield family in 1606 and remained with them until the late 18th century. In the 1780s it was leased, on his return from India, to William Byam Martin, who spent a great deal of money on improvements. In 1798 it was sold to the Marquis of

Blandford, later 5th Duke of Marlborough, a flamboyant and eccentric character who spent immense sums of money on converting the park into ornamental gardens, full of rare trees and exotic plants, rustic pavilions, fountains and grottoes. Whiteknights became a show-place, attracting many admiring and astonished visitors.

In Whiteknights House the Marquis assembled a magnificent collection of old masters and a library of early-printed books, which was recognised as one of the finest private collections in the country. Nearly 20 years of extravagant, and no doubt enormously enjoyable, expenditure brought him to financial ruin, and in 1819 all the contents of his house, gardens and conservatories were sold. The house, deserted when the Duke moved to Blenheim, was pulled down in 1840. The park survived and became, in 1947, the property of Reading University.

Two other ancient estates were those of Erleigh Court and Whitley Park. The latter had belonged to Reading Abbey until the Dissolution and had since passed through many hands. The former belonged in the late 18th century to John Bagnall, Esq., one of whose daughters married Sir William Scott, afterwards Lord Stowell, a distinguished man of law. Lord Stowell spent the last years of his life at Erleigh Court and died there in 1836.

At Woodley, Bulmershe manor had also once belonged to Reading Abbey but had passed to a branch of the Blagrave family. In 1777 a house called Woodley Lodge, later Bulmershe Court, was built there by James Wheble of Kensington. This house was purchased in 1789 by the Rt. Hon. Henry Addington, Speaker of the House of Commons, who became Prime Minister in 1801 and Viscount Sidmouth in 1805. Addington used Woodley Lodge as a summer residence, but after he became Prime Minister he sold it back to the Wheble family, in whose possession it remained for over a century.

The War
Against Napoleon

The year 1802 saw the publication of the first detailed description of Reading and the first account of its past history and achievements in an impressive volume entitled *The History and Antiquities of Reading.* The author was the Rev. Charles Coates, at that time Vicar of Osmington in Dorset and Chaplain to the Prince of Wales, to whom the book was dedicated. Coates was a native of Reading, having been born here some 56 years previously and having attended Reading School before going to Cambridge University. His *History,* compiled with immense care and labour from original manuscripts in the British Museum and elsewhere, had taken him ten years to write.

When it was published, Reading was approaching the end of its existence as a medium-sized market town and was about to enter upon a period of commercial and industrial expansion which, by 1900, would change it almost beyond recognition.

The Reading Coates described was "a handsome borough town, situated on the Bath Road ... surrounded, to the North, with rich meadows washed by the Thames, having a beautiful view extending from Mapledurham to Sunning." The map included in his book shows that, in size and shape, the town had hardly altered since John Speed drew his map nearly 200 years before. Most of it was still enclosed within the triangle formed by Friar Street in the north and the meeting place of Silver Street and Southampton Street in the south. Town's End was at the western end of Friar Street, beyond which lay the fields of Battle Farm and the road leading to Pangbourne, lined with trees and hedges. It was the same at other exits from the town. Once past the turnpike at the top of Castle Hill or Whitley Hill the traveller was in open country. Along London Road, past the Turk's Head, only a few scattered houses interrupted a view on both sides of cultivated fields and orchards, so that a stroll out to the Marquis of Granby Inn at the junction of the London and Forest Roads was a popular summer evening pastime.

By the end of the 19th century all this had changed. Reading had expanded to east and west, its new housing developments sprawling towards Earley and Tilehurst, and the new borough boundaries extending far beyond those described by Coates. The dashing Bath Road he knew had become a neglected rural highway, superannuated since the building of the railways, but lingering on as a reminder to imaginative novelists and topographers of the romance of the coaching age. Coates' rich meadows washed by the Thames, had been carved up and obliterated by an expanse of iron rails and blackened sleepers; while the foreground of the once famous view from Forbury Hill featured signal posts, engine sheds and station buildings — not to mention the trains. By 1901 the population of Reading had grown to more than 72,000. In Coates' lifetime, at the first official census taken in 1801, it numbered 9,742.

In the early years of the 19th century, England was at war with the French, a nation which, under Napoleon, had become the most powerful and most efficiently organised enemy this country had yet encountered. Although the war was fought at sea and in foreign lands, invasion scares brought its realities home to everyone. Even in households where no member of the family was away fighting, Bonaparte was the terrible bogey man, the threat of whose coming could be used to frighten naughty children into instant obedience.

In Reading, although so far inland, people were soon familiar with the sound of the drum, the sight of uniformed soldiers, and, as the war dragged on, the presence in the town of prisoners of war of various nationalities.

Early in the war two companies of volunteers had been raised in Reading, about two hundred men coming forward to take up arms for home defence. The first company, an association of gentlemen, was formed in 1794 with the declared object of maintaining peace and order in Reading and the countryside around it within a radius of six miles. In 1795 a second company was formed of townsmen who could not afford the expense of uniforms or the loss of working hours. They were therefore provided with uniforms by public subscription and paid by the Government at the rate of two shillings a week for their attendance.

Another local volunteer corps was the Woodley Cavalry, founded by the Rt. Hon. Henry Addington of Woodley Lodge. Addington took an active part in the preparations for defence, helping to raise subscriptions to augment the amount brought in by taxation, and himself contributing £2,000 to the fund. The Woodley Cavalry

The Three Tuns at Earley, which in the late 18th century was a meeting place of the Woodley Cavalry.

consisted of three officers and 54 men. Addington was in command; Edward Golding of Maiden Erlegh was Captain; Richard Palmer of Holme Park, Sonning, was Lieutenant. Among the privates were members of such well-known county families as the Blagraves, Simonds, Moncks and Whebles. The Woodley Cavalry used some old cottages in Church Road, Earley, as their barracks, and the nearby Three Tuns inn was the scene of their more convivial meetings.

In 1798, when the country was under serious threat of invasion, Reading responded by raising three more companies of volunteers. In August that year all the Reading Volunteers and the Woodley Cavalry were assembled on Bulmershe Heath to be presented with their colours by Mrs Addington. A sermon was preached at the consecration of the colours by Dr Valpy, Chaplain to both volunteer associations.

In the following summer, again on Bulmershe Heath, George III reviewed the local volunteer forces. It was an occasion of some splendour. Also present were the Queen, the Dukes of York and Cumberland, the five Princesses, the Prime Minister (William Pitt) and the Margravine of Anspach. The royal party spent the morning with the Addingtons at Woodley Lodge, refreshments being provided in a tent on the lawn. After the review the King praised the general fitness of the forces arrayed for his inspection.

The threat of invasion passed, and on the declaration of peace in 1802 the Reading Volunteers were disbanded and their colours hung in St Laurence's Church. But when, in 1803, it became clear that the peace had been only a breathing space to enable Napoleon to make further preparations for the conquest of England, war was again declared and the volunteer forces were hastily reassembled.

In the later years of the war the demand for men for the regular army was so great that recruiting stations were set up in towns and villages all over the country. In Reading five public houses in London Street were taken over for this purpose, the Black Horse and the Barley Mow being used as recruiting stations for the cavalry, while three others were for the line regiments. Most of the men recruited were wagoners and farm servants who had come into Reading for the market, and were persuaded by the recruiting parties, with the aid of tankards of free beer, to enlist. Many tricks were played on simple young men to get them to take the King's shilling; many attempts to escape were made by unwilling recruits, and many mothers and wives tried to buy a son's or husband's liberty. On one occasion a reluctant recruit made good his escape by jumping up onto one of the Bath coaches which had stopped at the corner of London Street, and was driven away to safety.

Apart from troops marching through the town Reading people also saw large numbers of prisoners of war. In 1800 bands of 300 and 600 French prisoners passed through Reading, and in 1813 another large party, in a wretched state, was escorted down London Street and lodged in the stables at the Saracen's Head Inn. An eye-witness recorded that their clothes were in rags and their shoes almost worn out. While they were in Reading some of the local people took pity on them, one or two talking to them in their own language. Some of the prisoners passed the time by carving mutton bones into small curiosities, such as domino boxes and tobacco stoppers, which they sold for a few pence to the townspeople.

Prisoners of other nationalities included Dutch, German, Norwegian and Danish. In 1814 Norwegian prisoners of war thanked Mr J.B. Monck, of Coley, for his public protest against the blockade of their country by the British fleet. Some of the Danish prisoners were particularly wretched, two of them committing suicide. Another of them died, but his name is recorded on a memorial tablet on the outer wall of St Mary's Church. He was Laurentius Braag, aged 25, a prisoner of war on parole in Reading, who died on 3 September 1808. More fortunate prisoners remained long enough in Reading to make friends among the local people, some of whom were sorry to see them depart when the war ended.

With Napoleon banished to Elba, peace came for a while in 1814. In July the town was brilliantly illuminated, and a gigantic dinner was laid on for the thousands of the poorer townspeople. No less than 80 tables were set in the streets, extending from the top of London Street down to Friar Street. Roast and boiled beef, veal pies and hot plum puddings were provided in abundance, followed by gallons of beer. No doubt the people deserved it. After so many years of war the nation's economy was in a bad way. The war had to be paid for, and the poor, as usual, were suffering from the high price of food and rising unemployment. Sick and wounded soldiers returning from the war added to the sum of the town's distress. Barely a year later, there were less extravagant festivities, and more sober thanksgivings, to mark the final defeat of Napoleon at Waterloo.

Reform

In the 1830s the cause of reform was nowhere more enthusiastically supported than in Reading.

The decade opened with a great deal of public agitation over the Bill for the reform of Parliament, which had long been an object with the more thoughtful and responsible section of the population. The burdens of all-pervading taxation, signs of wasteful and corrupt administration, the traditional ascendency in politics of the upper classes, were among the many grievances which had led to nationwide discontent. Worst of all, only a small proportion of the population had the right to vote at elections. In Reading in 1830 the electorate consisted of about 1,200 out of a population of nearly 16,000. By long tradition these fortunate, or unfortunate, few were subject to all kinds of bribery, corruption, threats and even violence from, or on behalf of, candidates seeking their votes. Disorderly scenes and drunkenness were the common accompaniments of election campaigns.

The introduction into Parliament of the Reform Bill in 1831 roused the interest of the whole country. In Reading several public meetings were held in support of the Bill, and when, early on the morning of 23 March, an express coach brought the news that the Bill had passed the Commons by a majority of one, there were scenes of rejoicing in the streets. The *Mercury,* staunchly Liberal and a champion of reform, printed 4,000 handbills to announce the good news, and several gentlemen volunteered to mount their horses straightway and deliver the handbills to the surrounding villages.

A majority of one, however, was too small. The Reform Bill was withdrawn, and reintroduced later that year after a parliamentary election in which the country returned a great majority of candidates who were in favour of the bill. In September it was passed in the Commons with a majority of 109, and again the delight of the nation was wholeheartedly shared by the people of Reading.

The town's celebrations were made memorable by the action of one Jerry Tibble, who was often employed on festive occasions to fire a cannon which stood in the Forbury. On this particular day, egged on by the youth of the town and encouraged by several glasses of wine, Jerry dragged the cannon up to the top of London Street and positioned it near the Crown Inn, where some Whigs were enjoying a celebration dinner. Then, to the delight of the local youths, and apparently forgetting that the cannon was already loaded, Jerry rammed in another cartridge and looked round for the order to fire. "Fire away, my man," said a gentleman standing at a window, and Jerry did fire. The cannon exploded, shattering glass in all the windows at the top of London Street and bringing people rushing from their houses thinking that there was an earthquake. Fortunately no-one, not even Jerry, was much hurt, but the cannon was blown to pieces and Jerry had some difficulty in escaping from a mob of angry householders.

Jerry's dramatic salute to the new age of reform was a little premature, for the bill was not passed in the Lords until June 1832, but the later date provided an excuse for further rejoicings. At dawn on 18 July cannon boomed (this time in orthodox fashion from the Forbury), drums beat, church bells rang, and people decorated their houses with laurel boughs. In London Street, as in every other main street in the centre of Reading, long tables were set up and loaded with food. At three o'clock 7,000 people sat down to dine, the vast banquet being presided over by John Berkeley Monck of Coley, a reformer who had represented Reading in three parliaments. Many of the onlookers joined in the feast, even genteel people partaking of the plum puddings and pronouncing them excellent.

Although the Reform Act did not immediately put an end to bribery (such as the influencing of tenants by landlords, or of shopkeepers by wealthy customers), it greatly increased the electorate, and in boroughs such as Reading gave the right to vote to every man who owned or occupied premises worth £10 a year.

The act had not long been passed when Liberal opinion began to urge reforms in local government, and a body of commissioners was set up to enquire into the administration of boroughs in England and Wales. Reading Corporation was among the authorities which came in for some sharp criticism. Its membership was confined to a small clique, to whom alone belonged the right to elect new members when vacancies occurred. Its 12 aldermen and 12 assistants held office for life, with the result that the town's affairs had been in the hands of a few powerful families for 50 years or more. The limited scope of its activities was indicated by its officers. These were a recorder, two treasurers, a town clerk (who also served as coroner), three sergeants at mace, a bridewell keeper and a town crier. The mayor also acted as clerk of the market and returning officer at elections.

By long tradition the Corporation administered its properties and its charities, but concerned itself very little with matters such as public health and safety, which were of vital importance to the whole community. Not surprisingly, the people of Reading were reported as viewing with jealousy and dissatisfaction the conduct of a body over whose membership and activities they had almost no control.

In 1835 the findings of the commissioners bore fruit when the Municipal Corporations Act swept away the old order and brought in a new style of governing body, whose members were elected by the townspeople and which, in time, was able to provide all the services needed by a fast growing population.

Meanwhile, in this extremely busy period of reform, another body of commissioners had been enquiring into provisions for the care of the nation's poor and unemployed, responsibility for which had rested with the parishes since the reign of Elizabeth I. The system had long been due for overhaul.

The 18th and early 19th centuries had seen a tremendous increase in the numbers of unemployed, caused by changes in agricultural and manufacturing methods, and the economic strain of long foreign wars. In 1816 a Reading diarist noted that the labouring class of people were in a most deplorable state; the poor houses were filled, and the Overseer's door was surrounded from morning till night by miserable objects seeking relief.

By the 1830s the situation had improved, but the cost of maintaining the poor continued to rise, and, in Reading, the poor rate amounted to £12,000 a year. Those "on the parish", either in the poor houses or in receipt of outdoor relief, were doing quite nicely. The trouble was that they were better off than independent labourers struggling to support themselves and their families on inadequate wages.

The makeshift poor-house in the former church of Greyfriars had long ago been replaced by three separate parish poor-houses, St Laurence's being at the western end of Friar Street, St Mary's in Pinkneys Lane and St Giles' in Southampton Street. The report of the Poor Law Commissioners on these institutions, particularly with regard to the extravagance of the allowances and the lack of employment for the inmates, attracted a good deal of public attention, and confirmed the worst suspicions of the ratepayers.

In reply to a question about the quantity of food provided, the governor of St Laurence's poor-house exclaimed, "Quantity! Why, a bellyful. We never stint them." Beer was allowed daily and meat three times a week. The poor-house was clean and well-kept; its inmates strong and healthy. Even the able-bodied among them did no work, but passed their days in idleness. They found their lot so agreeable, reported the governor, that "in general they never leave us." The account books showed that paupers receiving outdoor relief were also quite well-off, the money they were given for no work being almost as much as employers were paying to independent labourers.

At St Giles' and St Mary's poor-houses the picture was equally rosy. At St Giles' each man was allowed 21 pints of beer a week, and each woman or child 10 pints. The Vicar of St Mary's declared that the families in receipt of the most relief were the worst in his parish. It was remarked that when people were once on the parish or in the poor-house, they were never got off except by death.

The Poor Law Amendment Act of 1834 was designed to change all that. The old and sick were still to have a place of comparative comfort, but able-bodied paupers were no longer to be as well-off as working men. Reading's three poor-houses were combined under one Board of Guardians. St Giles' closed. St Mary's was used as the poor house for the borough. St Laurence's was converted into a workhouse for the able-bodied by the installation of two corn mills and a grain dressing machine. A rigid diet of two meals a day, the enforcement of strict discipline, and little contact with the outside world were all intended to discourage the poor from applying for workhouse relief.

In this same decade, reform also did away with the dozen or so watchmen who patrolled the streets at night, calling out the time and the state of the weather, and keeping as far away as possible from any sign of trouble. As preventers of crime they were as good as useless, even though the public were supposed to assist them in dealing with breaches of the peace. Street fights, drunkenness, burglary and robbery with violence were common in the town, while, on the outskirts, coaches, horsemen and carriages were frequently stopped and robbed.

In 1836 the watchmen were replaced by the newly created Borough Police Force. This consisted, at first, of 30 constables, two sergeants and two inspectors, by whose efforts a state more closely resembling law and order was brought to Reading.

The Coming
of the Railways

Until the railways were built travel and transport depended upon roads and waterways, and the expansion of commercial and industrial enterprises in the 18th and early 19th centures would not have been possible without advances in road and canal engineering which brought both means of communication to a high level of efficiency. Their great drawbacks were that both depended upon the power of the horse and the state of the weather; the waterways, in particular, being adversely affected by drought, flood and frost.

Because both roads and waterways passed through Reading, the centre of commercial activity had remained in the heart of the town. This was an aspect of the town's life which was to be radically changed when the railway was built across empty land on the northern side.

In the early decades of the 19th century the roads were busier than they had ever been before. The turnpike trusts, which had been set up in the previous century, collected from travellers, at strategically placed gates, tolls which were used for the upkeep of the roads. Their enterprise had brought about a countrywide improvement in road maintenance, and the smoother surfaces, made even more enjoyable by better sprung and upholstered vehicles, encouraged more people to travel for pleasure as well as on business.

On the roads converging upon Reading there were turnpikes at the top of Castle Hill on the Bath and Bristol Road, in Whitley Street on the road from Basingstoke and Southampton, at the top of Redlands Road near its junction with Shinfield Road, in Oxford Road just beyond the present site of Battle Hospital, and on the eastern side of Loddon Bridge where the old Forest Road linked up with the road from Wokingham and Bracknell.

In 1834 access to the eastern side of Reading was improved by the opening of King's and Queen's Roads (the relevant King and Queen being William IV and Adelaide), built on lands which had formerly belonged to the Crown.

Along these roads traffic of all kinds streamed into Reading, where the coaches and carriages brought business to the larger inns, while the carriers, wagoners, drovers and other humble travellers sought accommodation and companionship at the many smaller inns which flourished in the town.

Every weekday several coach services ran from Reading to London, some via Maidenhead and Slough, others via Wokingham, Bracknell and Staines. Regular coach services also ran to Abingdon and Oxford, Southampton, and Newbury, Bath and Bristol. The fast services to London were of material value to the Reading businessman, enabling him to travel to the City, transact business, and return home again within the day. They also made possible the carriage of perishable goods; fresh fish, for instance, bought at Billingsgate in the morning, could be on sale in the streets of Reading by two o'clock in the afternoon.

The waterways, enjoying the busiest and most prosperous years of their existence before the railways robbed them of their trade, still monopolised the carriage of heavy goods. The completion of the Kennet and Avon Canal in 1810, linking the Avon with the Thames, had created a continuous route between London and Bristol, and increased the prosperity of towns such as Newbury and Reading through which it passed.

The waterways network in England, was, by that time, well developed, but new canals were still being proposed to extend and improve it. Some, such as the proposed canal from Maidenhead to the Grand Junction Canal near Uxbridge, were intended to cut out the worst stretches of the Thames.

The river between Reading and London was by far the most troublesome part of the route, the navigation conditions being nowhere as good as those on the canal. Summer droughts and winter floods could make the journey dangerous, sometimes impossible. Barges could be held up for days or even weeks, causing inconvenience, extra expense and hardship to many people. In the autumn of 1814, when drought had so reduced the water level that no barges were able to get through for more than a month, Reading grocers were compelled to employ local carriers to bring goods by road from London, at nearly three times the cost of carriage by water.

Another seasonal problem on the waterways was frost. In the severe winter of 1813-14 a prolonged spell of frost and snow froze the canal, delaying much-needed supplies of coal, and putting bargemen out of

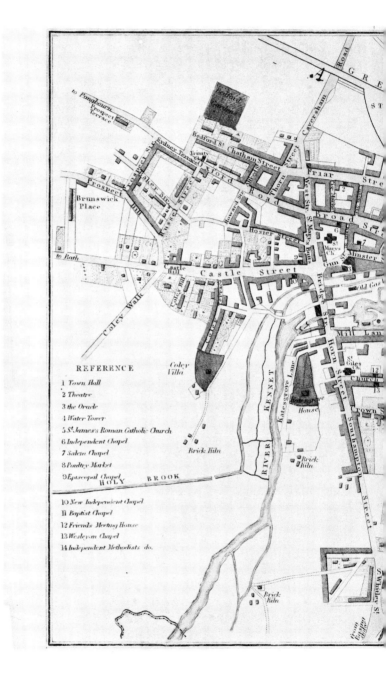

REFERENCE

1 Town Hall
2 Theatre
3 the Oracle
4 Water Tower
5 St. James's Roman Catholic Church
6 Independent Chapel
7 Salem Chapel
8 Poultry Market
9 Episcopal Chapel

10 New Independent Chapel
11 Baptist Chapel
12 Friends Meeting House
13 Wesleyan Chapel
14 Independent Methodists do.

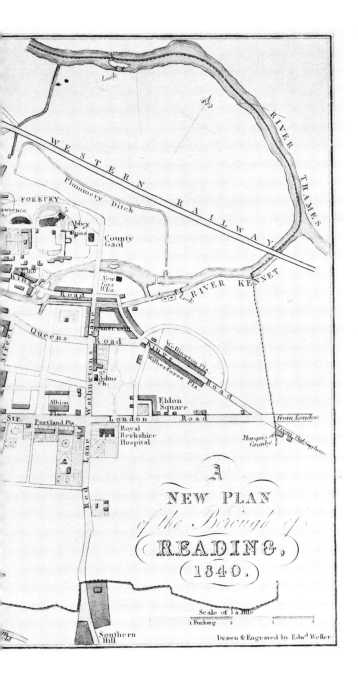

A

NEW PLAN

of the Borough of

READING,

1840.

Scale of ½ a Mile

Drawn & Engraved by Edw.d Weller.

work. Some of them were reduced to drawing a boat around the town, begging.

Delays of this kind inevitably caused problems all along the waterway, one dire result being that goods despatched from Bristol by water had sometimes to be unloaded at Reading wharves and sent on by road to London. Eventually, it was the frustrated merchants of Bristol who began to look for an alternative means of transport.

The invention of the steam engine and the success in the north of England of the first railways naturally attracted their attention, and in 1832 a committee was formed to consider the possibility of a railway between Bristol and London. In the following March Isambard Kingdom Brunel, designer of the Clifton Suspension Bridge, was appointed Engineer and instructed to make a survey of the route. In July 1833 his proposals were put forward and approved at a public meeting in Bristol Guildhall, and it was decided that a company should be formed and application made to Parliament for powers to build a railway.

In September readers of the *Reading Mercury* were able to study the prospectus of the Great Western Railway, and the wealthier ones among them to consider buying some of the £100 shares which were being advertised to raise the required capital of £3,000,000.

The proposed railway was the subject of months of heated controversy. Those in favour of it enumerated the advantages to be gained from speedy, cheap and safe transport for passengers and goods, the immense possibilities for expanding trade, the creation of years of employment for the labouring classes, and the enhanced value of properties in the neighbourhood of the railway. Opposition came loudly and vehemently from those who stood to lose by the railway; the canal and coach proprietors, the Thames Commissioners, the land-owners whose estates would be cut up and whose farms ruined by the construction of the line, and from a few towns which felt that the railway would not serve their best interests.

Reading was not one of these. From the beginning public opinion in the town was generally favourable and the pro-Liberal *Reading Mercury* supported the idea with enthusiasm. The opinions of the opposition were equally strongly expressed by a rival newspaper, the *Berkshire Chronicle,* which had been founded in 1825 as the organ of local Conservatism.

In December a great anti-railway meeting was held at the Bear Inn, attended by more than 30 Berkshire landowners and representatives from the Thames Commissioners. It was unanimously decided that the railway would be injurious to their interests and that no case of public utility could be made out to justify such an encroachment upon private property. But the general public was showing great interest in an exhibition at Reading Town Hall of detailed plans of the railway, and in March 1834 a public meeting was held there to listen to an informative speech by the Secretary of the Great Western Railway Company. His arguments were so convincing that, at the end of the meeting, it was decided to draw up a petition in favour of the railway and to ask Charles Russell, one of Reading's M.Ps, to present it in Parliament.

A few days later the first Great Western Railway Bill was introduced in the House of Commons, but although it was well supported there it was rejected by the House of Lords. A second Bill, put forward in the summer of 1835, proved successful. On the last day of August the *Mercury* triumphantly announced the good news and congratulated the townspeople on the achievement of their wishes.

Construction of the line began in February 1836. Just over two years later the first section as far as Maidenhead was completed and the station opened in June 1838. A year later the line had reached Twyford. Meanwhile work had been in progress since 1836 on the cutting, nearly two miles long and 60 feet deep, which had to be excavated between Twyford and Reading. This was to prove one of the most difficult sections of the work, requiring the labours of hundreds of navvies and a good many horses for nearly three years. Conditions were often appalling, particularly when heavy rain reduced the site to a sea of mud. Landslides on the embankments were common and caused the deaths of several men and horses. It was not until the end of 1839 that the way was clear for the line to be completed as far as Reading.

The opening of Reading Station took place at the end of March 1840. On 14 March a preliminary ceremony was held when Brunel and a party of Great Western company directors travelled down the line on a trial run from London, their arrival in Reading being watched and cheered by crowds of enthusiastic onlookers.

On 24 March public rejoicings were marred by an accident which killed one of the men working on the new station buildings. Henry West, a young journeyman carpenter, was working on the roof of the station shed when a sudden violent gust of wind tore off part of the roof, with the terrified man clinging to it, and hurled it to the ground some distance away. He was buried in St Laurence's churchyard, where his grave may still be seen. A memorial board put up by his fellow workmen records his strange death in a whirlwind.

On 30 March the station was opened for public use. Thousands of people flocked into Reading, many having travelled from distant towns and villages to see the wonderful new means of locomotion. Some came to ride on the trains, but most to watch, either from the seats lined up on the station platforms or from Forbury Hill or any available vantage point. Trains began to run at six o'clock in the morning and during the day 17 trains were to be seen arriving and departing, carrying numerous passengers. One of the afternoon trains brought Charles Russell, the former M.P. and now Chairman of the Great Western Railway Company.

Great excitement was caused by the speed of the trains, one of them taking only one hour and five minutes to accomplish the journey from London to Reading. This was less than a quarter of the time taken by the fast coach services. It was clear that the old way of travel was doomed.

In June 1841 the railway from London to Bristol was completed and it was the turn of the city merchants to celebrate the success of the enterprise.

The Victorian Expansion

The railway was an instant success as a means of passenger travel as well as for the conveyance of goods, but its effects were disastrous upon canal and river transport and upon the hundreds of inns whose livelihood had depended upon travel by slow stages.

In Reading the larger inns strove to attract customers by sending vehicles to meet all trains, but the opening in 1844 of the Great Western Hotel opposite the station further reduced their trade. The Bear and the Crown, both considerably enlarged during the years of their prosperity, were soon standing half empty and eventually, like many smaller inns, were closed.

Coach services kept going for some years on short distance journeys, and many operators ran special services to the nearest railway stations, but the long distance coaches very soon gave up trying to compete with the railway. The last stage coach from London to Bristol ran in 1843.

The waterways were equally hard hit, the Kennet and Avon losing nearly all its through traffic immediately after the completion of the line to Bristol. Its receipts from tolls fell from £51,000 in 1840-1 to less than £40,000 in 1841-2. But, as with the coach services, local traffic on the canals continued for some years.

The railway network quickly expanded. Branch lines were built to other towns which wanted to share the benefits of the new means of communication, and along each line hitherto remote villages were brought within easy reach of towns and of London itself. In 1847 the line from Reading through the Kennet valley to Newbury and Hungerford was completed. In 1848 the Great Western at Reading was linked with the South Western Railway from London to Southampton at Basingstoke. In 1849 Reading South Eastern station opened with a line connecting Reading with the Guildford and Reigate system at Farnborough, and in 1856 the completion of the line between Wokingham and Staines provided Reading with a second railway link

The Great Western and South Eastern Railway stations at Reading, about 1849.

with London via Waterloo.

The enormous benefits offered by railways to trade and industry were soon to be seen in the rapid expansion of two local firms, Sutton & Sons, and Huntley & Palmers, both founded in the 19th century and both destined to become world famous.

The foundations of Sutton's were laid in 1807 when John Sutton set up in business in Reading as a corn and seed merchant. In the 1830s his son, Martin Hope Sutton, an enthusiastic botanist and gardener, started a trial seed ground and achieved such good results that Sutton's display of tulips in 1835 excited great admiration. In 1837 Martin Hope decided to set up his own business and persuaded his father to join him under the title of John Sutton & Son.

The new firm settled in premises on the eastern side of Market Place, a site which was well chosen. Their shop fronted onto an area which was crowded with farmers and country people on market days and with shoppers on other days. At the back there was a garden, originally one of the gardens of Reading Abbey, and now a vital feature of the newly established business.

Martin Hope's initiative, expertise, business ability and fair dealing were to win for Sutton's an ever expanding market. He was quick to take advantage of the cheap and speedy transport provided by the newly instituted penny post as well as by the railways to extend his trade to all parts of the country. In 1840 he began to send out, free of

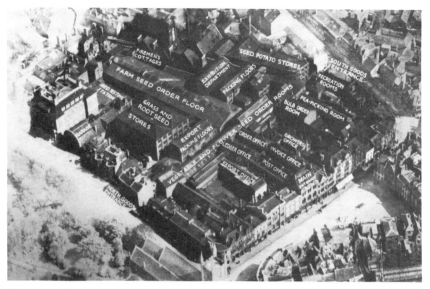

Sutton's at Reading, showing the extent of the Royal Seed Establishment to the east of Market Place, about 1920.

charge, catalogues containing notes for amateurs on the proper methods of cultivating flowers and vegetables, an innovation which proved tremendously valuable and encouraging to gardeners. His catalogues of agricultural seeds made his products, including many entirely new varieties, widely known to British farmers, and a further inducement to customers to order from Sutton's was his practice of sending goods carriage paid — another of his new ideas.

The reputation of the firm for quality and reliability was established by his determined campaign against the widespread practice of adulterating seed supplies with inferior or dead seeds. It was largely due to his efforts that Parliament eventually passed an Act against seed adulteration. Every consignment of every variety of seeds sold by Sutton's was subjected to searching tests, so that only those with a high germinating power were sold. The happy result was that Sutton's customers enjoyed much better harvests than their neighbours, and Sutton's business increased until it became the largest of its kind in the world. The export trade in seeds had at one time suffered from the deterioration caused by transit through the tropics, but here again Sutton's enterprise and expertise perfected a system whereby seeds could be sent to all parts of the world with their vitality uninjured by the journey.

As suppliers of seeds to royal farms and gardens Sutton's called their Reading headquarters The Royal Seed Establishment. By the end of the century their offices, stores, order rooms, loading floors and stable block covered nearly six acres, extending into Kings Road, Abbey Square and the Forbury. The original garden had been replaced by extensive trial grounds and a testing station on the outskirts of Reading, nicely situated to meet the eyes of travellers into the town along the Great Western and South Eastern railways. Sutton's magnificent exhibits were highlights at agricultural and horticultural shows all over England.

Like Sutton's, Huntley & Palmers owed its origins to a well-established but modest family business. In 1822 Joseph Huntley opened a biscuit bakery and confectioner's shop in Reading, he himself managing the business while his son, Thomas, did the baking. The shop, at 72 London Street, was quite small. The family lived above it and the bakehouse was in the cellar underneath.

On the opposite side of London Street stood the Crown Inn, Reading's largest posting inn, where several coaches a day stopped to change horses and allow the passengers to stretch their legs and to buy something to eat and drink if they wished. As the time allowed was usually too short for a meal at the inn many travellers preferred to stroll across the road to buy biscuits at Mr Huntley's shop. Joseph naturally encouraged this trade, and sent a boy over to the Crown with a basket of biscuits to sell to travellers waiting on the coaches or in the inn yard.

The biscuits, in the early years, were sold loose and had to be eaten fairly quickly, but after a while Joseph hit upon the idea of packing them in tin boxes, so that they would keep fresh and whole for some time. His younger son (also Joseph) who was in business as an ironmonger next door to the Crown, was persuaded to make the necessary boxes. In this way was founded the tin box firm of Huntley Boorne & Stevens, whose decorative tins were to carry Huntley & Palmers' biscuits all over the world.

For Joseph Huntley the potential market for biscuits was no longer purely local. By the 1830s he was despatching them by the well-organised canal system to towns and villages throughout southern and central England. By that time Thomas was making about 20 different varieties, ranging from plain Abernethys and Olivers to the more fancy macaroons and ratafias. He also made several kinds of cakes and buns.

Ill-health forced Joseph to retire in 1838. Thomas, although a good baker, lacked the business ability to carry on alone. In 1841 he went into partnership with George Palmer, a young man who had not long completed his apprenticeship as a miller and confectioner and had recently come to Reading.

In this partnership Huntley's craftsmanship and insistence on the highest standards were combined with Palmer's flair for business. Palmer's energy, initiative and interest in mechanisation were to transform a thriving family concern into the biggest biscuit enterprise in the world. Although the junior partner he was, from the start, effectively in control. Within a year he had doubled the size of the establishment by taking over the shop next door and introduced into the bakehouse a steam powered machine for mixing dough. In collaboration with William Exall, a Reading iron founder, he invented machinery for speeding up the manufacture of bisuits. In 1846, owing to his initiative, the firm moved to larger premises in King's road, taking over a factory built in 1841 for a silk manufacturer whose business had failed.

King's Road, built in the 1830s, was then a developing area between the town centre and the junction of the London and Wokingham Roads. The new factory was situated between the River Kennet and the new canal cut, while the Great Western Railway was only a few hundred yards to the north. Several other factories stood nearby, including the Cannon Brewery and the Gas Works.

On a site of half an acre George Palmer had space to try out his revolutionary ideas in factory management and in the use of continuously moving and integrated machinery. By the 1860s Huntley & Palmers biscuit factory was the largest in England and acknowledged leader of the industry. It was then producing about 100 varieties of plain and fancy biscuits to cater for all tastes. The nation's biscuit consumption increased, particularly after the custom grew up among the well-to-do and leisured classes of taking afternoon tea — a custom which led to the opening of hundreds of ladies' tea-shops.

Biscuits also sustained travellers on long journeys in the years before restaurant cars were introduced on the railways in the 1890s. George Palmer missed no opportunity for advertisement. At Paddington Station first class passengers were given a small packet of biscuits in a neat wrapper bearing the instruction to look out for Huntley &

Palmers' works at Reading. The red-brick factory was a conspicuous feature, immediately identifying Reading for travellers approaching the town.

The firm began to deliver biscuits to Windsor Castle in the 1850s, and in 1867 their stationery began to bear the royal arms and the coveted phrase 'By Appointment to the Queen'. The popular Osborne biscuit was named after the royal residence on the Isle of Wight.

After Thomas Huntley's death in 1857 the firm was carried on by George Palmer and his two brothers, William Isaac, who managed the factory, and Samuel, who created the London Office and took over responsibility for buying ingredients as well as for overseas sales.

The original site in King's Road was enlarged by the acquisition of adjacent properties and new factories were built. The purchase of the former Blake's Wharf on the northern bank of the Kennet in the 1860s made possible the construction of another large factory with its own packing rooms and loading sheds, and of the firm's own railway sidings, linking the heart of the works with the main railway lines.

Hot biscuits being offered to coach travellers outside Huntley & Palmers' original shop in London Street.

The firm's output became so great that its requirements of high quality ingredients could no longer be supplied entirely from local sources. Flour, which at first had been supplied almost exclusively by Swallowfield Mill, was by the 1850s supplied also by Hurley and Whitchurch Mills, and by the 1870s in vast quantities from East Anglia. At his London office Samuel Palmer was responsible for buying millions of eggs and thousands of tons of butter from sources as far away as Belgium, Ireland, France and Spain.

Huntley & Palmers began exporting in the 1840s and were soon trading with the United States, India, China, Australia and Africa. Their biscuits were especially popular with civilian and military communities in all parts of the British Empire.

By the end of the 19th century Huntley & Palmers' employees numbered over 5,000; in 1846 the total had been 41. For several decades the firm was the largest employer of labour in Reading.

The tin box factory of Huntley Boorne & Stevens expanded along with Huntley & Palmers, supplying the tins so essential to the trade. The wonderful variety of pictures used to decorate the tins, showing the landscapes, peoples and customs of foreign countries (in all of which the famous firm's biscuits were clearly as popular as they were in England) made the tins desirable objects in their own right. After the process of offset-litho printing on tin was developed it was possible to print on curved surfaces, so that the tins could be made in many unusual and original shapes. From the 1880s until the Second World War Huntley & Palmers' novelty Christmas tins were an annual attraction. Huntley Boorne & Stevens remained in London Street until the 1960s, long outliving the old Crown Inn next door.

Two other local industries which achieved new heights of prosperity in the 19th century were iron founding and brick and tile making.

William Exall, who had helped George Palmer with his early mechanical experiments, was a member of the iron founding firm of Barrett, Exall & Andrewes. Their works, known as the Reading Iron Works after 1864, were in Katesgrove and, in course of time, expanded to both banks of the Kennet. By the 1870s they were widely known and highly regarded as makers of agricultural machinery; their steam engines and threshing machines won medals and diplomas at most important national and international exhibitions. Other successful lines were mowing and haymaking machines, ploughs and horse rakes.

Brick making had been carried on in Reading for centuries, the clay found on the hillsides above the Kennet being of good quality and easily worked. Kilns were established at Katesgrove, Coley and Tilehurst. At Katesgrove, by the late 19th century, the older kilns near the town were disused, but Waterloo Kilns were still busy producing bricks, tiles and drain pipes, while Rose Kilns further to the south were also active. At Coley, on the site of the present recreation ground, two firms were making bricks, tiles and pottery until the last quarter of the century, when both moved to Tilehurst.

Samuel Wheeler moved from Coley in 1885 and founded Tilehurst Potteries at Kentwood Hill, where he built up a very successful business in roofing tiles of various colours and flower pots, his products enjoying far more than a local reputation.

S. & E. Collier, the most famous of Reading's brickmakers, moved from Coley to Grovelands in lower Tilehurst. Their very extensive works produced bricks, tiles and terra cotta which placed Colliers' among the leading British manufacturers in this field. They remained in business until 1965.

Colliers' bricks may still be seen all over Reading, their many colours helping to create the infinite variety of patterns in brickwork which is so distinctive and lively a feature of the town's architecture.

The triumphant power and speed of the steam engine and the rapid advance of railway systems brought not only a means of speedier progress and expansion to commerce and industry but a widespread acceleration of activity among people to whom rail transport was available. Speedier transport and postal services encouraged speedier action. The possibility of visiting places and taking part in events far beyond the immediate locality encouraged a widening of people's interests and understanding. Trains were crowded not only with men of business but with the general public, eager to travel not only faster but further and more often.

Towns which were situated on main railway lines began to grow faster than towns which were not. Reading's old rivals, Wallingford and Abingdon, served only by branch lines built some years after the main lines, remained peaceful country market towns, by-passed by industry and showing little increase in size or population. At Reading the main line railways attracted industry, which in its turn attracted thousands of people in search of employment. The growing population demanded more and better public and professional services, and so drew more professional men to the town. Reading expanded quickly; its built-up area increased by streets of small terrace houses for the working classes, and roads lined with detached houses standing in

The Hop Fair held in the new Corn Exchange, on the west side of Market Place, in 1859.

spacious gardens for the professional classes and for other new residents who chose the town for its amenities and accessibility from London.

In 1832 and 1833 the Crown Estate to the east of Reading was put up for auction. The estate, which had belonged to the Crown since the dissolution of Reading Abbey, comprised most of the land between the Thames and London Road, extending eastwards as far as Cemetery Junction and westwards to Duke Street. The auctioneers, when appraising the desirability of plots on this land, were confident that the King's Road, recently built across it, would become the new high road to Bath and Bristol, by-passing the longer route via London Road and Southampton Street. This, they said, would make plots on the salubrious eastern section of the estate ideal for villas and other gentlemen's residences. The western section, where the King's Road ran between the River Kennet and the canal cut, would be suitable for shops, warehouses and factories.

The auctioneers were right in their expectation that the area would be one of mixed commercial and residential development, but King's Road was never to become the high road to Bristol (superannuated less than ten years later by the railway), and the canal's most enduring contribution to the area was the importation of loads of Bath stone to build the gentlemen's residences.

Further developments between the town and the Crown Estate were made possible by the sale, in 1833 and 1834, of land belonging to Reading Corporation and upon which Queen's Road, South Street and Sidmouth Street had just been laid out.

Some of the first houses to be built on these newly released lands were those around Eldon Square and Eldon Road, soon to become desirable residences for the growing medical staff at the Royal Berkshire Hospital nearby. Other good stone houses put up in the 1840s, either in pairs or in terraces, were built in King's Road, Victoria Square and Queen's Crescent. Nearer to the town centre the King's Road Baptist Church was opened in 1834.

Later housing developments in east Reading were on a more modest scale. Many side streets, such as Princes Street and St John's Road, contained small brick houses intended for working class people, and after 1880 the tremendous demand for workers' houses created by Huntley & Palmers and other industries led to the construction of networks of streets of terrace houses off London and Wokingham Roads. All were built of the cheap and readily available bricks made at Tilehurst and Katesgrove.

In addition, a great deal of church building took place. Those put up to serve this fast-growing area included St John's, Watlington Street, first built in 1837 and replaced by a larger building in 1872-3, St Stephen's, Orts Road, 1864-6, and St Bartholomew's, London Road, built in 1879 on a site presented by George Palmer. In Queen's Road, Trinity Congregational Church was built in 1846 and Wesley Chapel in 1873; while at the far end of King's Road Wycliffe Baptist Chapel was built in 1881. In London Road the Unitarian Church of 1878 and St Andrew's Presbyterian Church of 1880 were designed to serve the whole town.

To the south of London Road, and east of Redlands Road, the Redlands Estate was developed between the 1860s and the 1880s. Here a more uniformly pleasant residential area grew up, comfortably remote from the railway and untouched by commerce or industry. Here again the houses, whether large or small, were built of local brick, and so was St Luke's Church in Erleigh Road, opened in 1883.

Just beyond the Redlands Estate lay Whiteknights Park, where in 1868 the eminent Victorian architect, Alfred Waterhouse, bought a plot of land and built himself a house called Foxhill. Among the important public buildings he designed for Reading are the former Municipal Buildings and clocktower in Blagrave Street, opened in 1875, and the present Reading School in Erleigh Road, opened in 1871.

To the west of Redlands Road lay a piece of land which Reading Corporation had formerly owned, having purchased it out of John Kendrick's legacy. In 1849 this land was claimed by Christ's Hospital, London, in their successful suit against the Corporation for misuse of the Kendrick bequest. The name of a new road running across it, which the Corporation had originally called Victoria Street, was changed to Kendrick Road. In 1880-82 one of the finest houses in this area was built for William Isaac Palmer, on land in Allcroft Road which he leased from Christ's Hospital. It was named, very appropriately, Hillside, and was his home until his death in 1893.

Christ Church, magnificently placed at the top of the hill, was built in 1861-2 and enlarged in 1874.

Reading's other major area of expansion was on its western side. Quite early in the 19th century Chatham Street was built, continuing the line of Friar Street beyond the point which had long been known as Town's End. Further out along Oxford Road (in this century of widening horizons no long called Pangbourne Road) Russell Street, Prospect Street, Baker Street, Sydney Terrace and Prospect Terrace provided new town houses for the middle classes. Holy Trinity Church was opened in 1826.

Later developments enclosed this area in streets of brick terrace houses spreading out towards the railway lines to the north and west. Great Knollys Street was developed about 1850 when the new Cattle Market was built there. Its name was a reminder that the land had once been part of Battle Manor, owned by the Knollys family since the 16th century. On the western side of the branch line to Newbury, Battle Farm survived well into the 20th century. The new Westerns Elms estate, on the south side of Oxford Road, had its streets named after the Prince of Wales, and the Dukes of Edinburgh, Connaught and Albany, the four sons of Queen Victoria.

Further south, more spacious and exclusive residences were built along Bath Road and Southcote Road, where a variety of stone, brick and stuccoed villas stood in large, well-timbered gardens. This area, however, was too thinly populated to support the church which was built to serve it. All Saints', in Downshire Square, was first opened when partly built in 1864, and reopened when the nave and chancel were completed in 1874, but its intended spire was never added, owing to a shortage of funds and of new parishioners wanting to build on the vacant plots of land.

Public Health and Welfare in the 19th Century

While new areas of Reading had been growing up, changes and improvements had been taking place in the older parts of the town. Many of these were in the cause of public health, one of the great concerns in this century of increasing scientific knowledge and worsening evils brought about by the overcrowding in towns and cities.

As early as 1802 the Reading Dispensary, in Chain Street, was founded by a group of local doctors, with the object of providing advice and medicine, free of charge, to poor patients. In 1814 the Dispensary began to combat the ever-present scourge of smallpox by giving free vaccination to the poor. In the late 1830s it cared for many workmen injured during the construction of the Great Western Railway. The Dispensary was rebuilt in 1848, by which time it was dealing with about 1000 patients a year.

After May 1839 responsibility for treating the injured railwaymen was shared by the newly opened Royal Berkshire Hospital, to which the directors of the Great Western Railway Company donated 100 guineas after a particularly bad accident in Sonning cutting in July 1839.

The Hospital stood on land given for the purpose by Viscount Sidmouth (he who many years before had commanded the Woodley Cavalry and was now living at Erleigh Court), and the money for the building was raised by a public subscription well supported by the landed gentry of Berkshire. The architect of the original building (now the central section) with its magnificent Ionic portico was Henry Briant. The opening was celebrated with great public rejoicing marked by a splendid procession through the streets and a dinner with speeches at the Town Hall which lasted five hours. The Hospital's accommodation for 80 beds was soon under heavy pressure from far too many patients, some, owing to the new railway, being able to travel from distant parts of the county.

In 1841 the Reading Pathological Society was formed by members of the medical staff to promote the advancement of knowledge and interest in the art and science of medicine.

Among the public services introduced in the 19th century were gas lighting and a piped water supply. The Reading Gas Light Company was formed in 1818 and set up its works in Bridge Street near the coal wharves. During the following year gas lamps were installed in the main streets to replace the old oil lamps, and the new illumination was turned on for the first time on 5 November 1819. Everything went well for several years, the brighter lighting being praised as "not only ornamental but a great protection against nocturnal depredators." In the 1830s the Company came in for some criticism caused by a falling off in quality and rising prices, and a rival company was formed, called the Reading Union Gas Company, with works in Gas Lane. For some years keen competition between the two companies kept the price of gas very low, but it also kept down the companies' profits, and in 1862 the two were amalgamated into the more viable Reading Gas Company.

The public water supply took much longer to organise, the real necessity for a constant supply of pure water in every home being not fully appreciated until the middle of the century.

The town's earliest waterworks project had started in 1694, when an engine had been set up in Mill Lane to pump water into the town centre, but its power proved inadequate and it was abandoned. Not until another century had passed was the project revived, a more powerful engine installed and a leaden cistern placed in Broad Street, from which the water could be piped into the houses of people willing to pay for it. As the water was supplied, untreated, from a part of the Kennet downsteam from tanyards, brick kilns, iron works and innumerable gutter outlets there was no great rush of customers, most people preferring their old-fashioned well-water. The Water Company's reputation was further undermined by a high incidence of burst pipes, flooded streets and stoppages caused by fish and eels finding their way into the pipes.

In 1818 William Cubitt, civil engineer, advised a reconstruction of the works. Pumping machinery capable of raising 250,000 gallons a day was installed, a lofty tank tower was built in Mill Lane, and a second reservoir at Spring Gardens on Whitley Hill. These improvements enabled the water to reach the higher parts of the town. The tower in Mill Lane continued in use until after 1850, and remained a local landmark until 1901.

128

In 1826 Reading Corporation made another major effort to improve the town by obtaining from Parliament an act giving them greater powers for paving, lighting, cleansing and watching the borough. The lengthy and minutely detailed list of regulations and prohibitions contained in this act caused it to be laughingly described as the 'All-Perfection Act', but it achieved at least some improvement in the state of the streets and helped to get rid of many obstructions and nuisances. The commencement of a regular weekly collection of household rubbish as well as of the dirt and manure in the streets must have been a considerable benefit. The collectors' carts, which had to have the words 'Scavenger's Cart' painted on them in two-inch high Roman letters, were probably the first council vehicles on the streets.

It was not until the 1840s that any real attempt was made to deal with the worst of the health problems, the inadequate and unclean water supply and the almost non-existent arrangements for sewerage and drainage. Public protests by leading citizens and a lengthy enquiry, to which members of the medical profession contributed telling evidence, produced an appalling picture of life in the old town centre. Emphasis was laid upon the dozens of congested courts and narrow back streets where a large proportion of the population lived in close proximity to open cesspools, foul privies and stinking pigsties. In some places the already poisoned air was made almost unbearable by the stench from nearby slaughterhouses. Most of the population shared communal taps, to which the Water Company was able to supply water for only a few hours a day. Elsewhere, people drew water from wells contaminated by adjacent cesspools, or fetched it from the river some distance away.

Inevitably the people in these areas enjoyed, at best, a state of chronic ill-health. Medical men confirmed that outbreaks of cholera, typhoid fever, smallpox and scarlatina were common, and statistics showed that the death rate in Reading was far higher than in other parts of Berkshire. Even for the dead conditions were bad, as there was little chance of decent burial. The three ancient parish churchyards were so full of bodies that it was hardly possible to inter any more without disturbing previous corpses. People living in the neighbourhood of the churchyards complained of the noxious vapours arising from them, and of the gruesome sights revealed by the gravediggers' spades. A remedy for this particular problem had been provided in 1843, when the new cemetery was opened at the junction of London and Wokingham Roads, but this had been little used, many people preferring the old burial grounds for sentimental and other reasons.

The recommendations made in a report to the newly created Board of Health in 1850 were thorough and comprehensive. The 'monster evil of the cesspool system' must be abolished and a complete and efficient system of underground drainage and sewage disposal laid down. There should be a constant supply of pure water to every house. Pigsties, slaughterhouses and other offensive buildings must be removed. Interment in the new cemetery must be compulsory. The streets should be given hard and durable surfaces which could be kept clean with water from conveniently placed hydrants. Public baths and wash-houses should be provided for the poor.

The Council and the Board of Health were not slow to act, and the next ten years were a period of unprecedented change. Major slum clearances were carried out; cesspools were filled in; the old burial grounds were closed; town centre slaughterhouses were abolished and properly organised abbattoirs were built beside the new Cattle Market in Great Knollys Street. The Council bought up the Reading Water-works Company and new works were built at Southcote Mill, two miles upstream from the town. Here the water was filtered before being pumped to a new reservoir excavated on the north side of Bath Road. In the 1870s new works were built at Fobney lock, capable of supplying the town for many years to come.

After the cleaning up process of the 1850s, the 1860s saw several cosmetic improvements to the face of the town, and some succesful attempts to preserve its historic buildings.

In 1862 the part of Broad Street adjoining King Street was at last cleared of the obstruction of Middle Row, the old Fisher and Butcher Rows which had formerly contained many slaughterhouses. In 1868 the northern end of Market Place lost an attractive feature by the demolition of the Blagrave Piazza, a covered arcade erected in 1619 along the south wall of St Laurence's Church with money bequeathed by John Blagrave.

The Forbury was transformed. This public open space, once the outer court of Reading Abbey, had long been used for fairs, cattle markets and other outdoor events. In 1831, Forbury Hill, then a popular vantage point for enjoying the view across the Thames Valley, had been beautified under the supervision of Joshua Vines, a resident of Friar Street, but the rest of the area was commonly used as a rubbish tip. Fortunately the Council's cleaning up operations in the 1850s were

Disappearing Reading. The junction of Broad Street and Minster Street before the old houses in Fisher Row and Butcher Row (left) were demolished. The George inn had not yet expanded into the property at the corner of Minster Street.

extended to the Forbury, and by 1861-2 the whole area was laid out with formal paths and flower gardens for the healthful recreation of the public.

At the same time the last ragged remains of Reading Abbey were tidied up and the site laid out to form a continuation of the garden walks. A living link with the past history of the abbey had been created in 1840 with the opening of the Catholic Church of St James, built partly on the site of the abbey church. Stones from the ruins had been used to help build the floor and walls of the new church and an

131

elaborately carved Norman capital, found in the ruins in 1835, was used to make the font.

The only part of the abbey to survive in a clearly recognisable state was the inner gateway, which had linked the outer court with the abbey proper. This too, was in a ruinous condition, and in 1861-2 was restored by the distinguished architect, 'Sir Gilbert Scott.

In the following year the last remaining part of the medieval friary was saved. Greyfriars Church, whose walls alone had survived nearly three centuries of misuse as a town hall, workhouse and prison, was purchased from the Corporation by public subscription, rebuilt, and consecrated in December 1863.

Another historic structure in danger of collapse was Caversham Bridge. This had been in existence since 1231 and had undergone innumerable repairs, some necessitated by deliberate destruction during the Civil Wars. Responsibility for its maintenance had always been divided; in earlier times between the Abbot of Reading and the Lord of the Manor of Caversham; in later times between the borough of Reading and the county of Oxfordshire. The result of centuries of piecemeal repairs was a bridge which was undeniably picturesque but laid no claims to strength or beauty. It consisted partly of stone, partly of brick, and partly of timber, and its arches were of various ill-assorted shapes and sizes. To make matters worse, the Caversham end was narrower than the Reading end. In 1868-9 this poor old bridge was taken down and replaced by a briskly utilitarian iron bridge. It lasted less than 60 years.

In 1867 a new Union Workhouse was opened in Oxford Road, occupying what was then described as a salubrious position about a mile from the town centre. It was designed to accommodate 250 persons and to replace the old parish institutions. In addition to the workhouse building for the poor and the physically and mentally handicapped, there was a separate hospital building for people suffering from contagious or infectious diseases. Some 50 years later this institution was to become Battle Hospital.

The Reading end of old Caversham Bridge shortly before the bridge was demolished in 1868-9.

The new iron Caversham Bridge built in 1868.

The 19th Century – 1870-1900

In the last 30 years of the 19th century civic pride in the achievements and progress of the town as a manufacturing, commercial and residential centre was plainly to be seen in the impressive and exuberant public buildings which were erected, in the monuments which were set up to mark great occasions or in honour of famous men, and in the innumerable banquets, ceremonies and celebrations whose glory and glitter have long passed from living memory. The buildings and the monuments remain.

The new Municipal Buildings completed in 1875 were designed by Alfred Waterhouse, who only a few years before had designed the magnificent and very much larger Town Hall at Manchester, and was to rise to the honoured position of President of the Royal Institute of British Architects. The new buildings involved the demolition of part of the 18th century building, leaving only the assembly hall standing. They provided a more spacious and ornate council chamber, offices for the growing number of officials needed for new local government services, and a suitably dignified entrance under a clock tower which was to become one of Reading's most distinctive architectural features. Local craftsmanship did justice to the architect's design. The red and grey bricks and terra cotta ornaments were made at Colliers' works. The new buildings were opened with much ceremony in 1876, the Lord Mayor of London being among the many dignitaries present.

Six years later the modest 18th century assembly hall was superseded by a very much larger hall capable of seating 1500 people and of accommodating orchestral concerts, civic banquets and many other grand occasions. Such a hall had long been needed in the town, where there were few halls of any kind and no hall suitable for major public entertainments. A popular addition to it was the Willis organ, which had been presented to the previous town hall by the Reading Philharmonic Society in 1864. Now considerably enlarged and set in an elaborately carved oak case, the organ was an impressive sight above the platform. A recital by Dr Walter Parratt of Magdalen College, Oxford, formed part of the opening ceremony in May 1882.

The new hall was only part of an extensive range of buildings, designed by Thomas Lainson, which was being added to the Municipal Buildings, and included a Public Library and Museum, opened in 1883-4. A third section, designed by W.R. Howell, and containing an extension to the Library and an Art Gallery, was added at the Valpy Street end and opened in 1897. All the additions were designed to harmonise with the original Waterhouse building, but were allowed a variety of decorative detail.

The Public Library, Museum and Art Gallery were paid for chiefly by public subscription, by far the most munificent donor being William Isaac Palmer, while Huntley & Palmers and Reading's M.P., Sir Francis Goldsmid, also contributed generously. William Isaac Palmer was one of the most active promoters of the scheme, which had not received much public support when it was first mooted in the 1870s. One of the ways in which he encouraged public interest in the idea was by running a small free library in West Street for several years until the Public Library was opened. He was Chairman of the Library and Museum Committee until his death in 1893.

Reading's civic pride and dignity received a tremendous boost when the borough boundaries were enlarged in 1887-9, and when, in 1888, Reading was granted County Borough status, confirming its rights of self-government and independence of Berkshire County Council.

The boundary extension doubled the size of the borough, which had remained unchanged since the reign of Elizabeth I, to more than 5,800 acres. Most of the new acreage was farm land to the south and west, taking in Whitley and Southcote. On the eastern side, the adjacent part of Earley beyond Cemetery Junction, which was already half covered with housing developments, was brought into the borough, and the new boundary ran out to its present limit along Church Road. On the Tilehurst side, Reading was extended a further half-mile to the west, bringing in part of Grovelands and Brock Barracks, built for the Royal Berkshire Regiment 10 years earlier, together with the garrison church of St George. The northern boundary along the Thames remained unchanged.

1886 and 1887 saw the unveiling of four of Reading's monuments. The Maiwand Lion, in the middle of the Forbury Gardens, was put up in memory of the 328 officers and men of the Royal Berkshire Regiment who died in a gallant rearguard action at Maiwand during

The Maiwand Lion memorial in Forbury Gardens, showing the original brick and terra cotta plinth which was later enclosed in the present stone plinth.

the Afghan Campaign of 1879-80. The monument was unveiled by Lord Wantage, with military and civic honours, in December 1886. The sculptor of this magnificent roaring lion, which measures 31 feet from nose to tail, was George Blackall Simonds, a member of the family owning Simonds' Brewery. He was to be commissioned to do two more monuments for the town within the next five years.

1887 was the year of Queen Victoria's Golden Jubilee, an event which inspired a tremendous outburst of loyal and patriotic fervour all over the country. There were civic ceremonies, street parties and celebrations of all kinds and, like many other towns, Reading decided to commission a statue of the Queen. George Simonds was called upon to produce a marble statue of Her Majesty in robes of state, which was placed in front of the new Municipal Buildings and unveiled by the Duke of Cambridge in July 1887. On the other side of the town, an elaborate two-tiered fountain, heavily decorated with patriotic emblems, was erected in St Mary's Butts and ceremoniously turned on by the Mayoress on 18 June. The fountain commemorated not only the Queen's Jubilee but a recently completed street improvement. St Mary's Butts, perhaps the oldest street in Reading, had become one of the seediest, and was disfigured by a row of dilapidated buildings in the centre. These had been cleared away and the area round St Mary's churchyard tidied up; the work having been done largely at the instigation and expense of a surgeon named Isaac Harrinson, who lived nearby in Castle Street. The parishioners recorded their thanks to him by causing a memorial in the form of a mediaeval cross to be erected in the churchyard. It was unveiled by the Vicar on Christmas Eve 1887.

Four years later Reading was again in festive mood in honour of George Palmer, J.P., M.P. for Reading 1878-85, and head of the town's greatest industry. He was also the town's greatest benefactor. In 1875 he had given 14 acres of King's Meadows, beside the Thames, for use as a public recreation ground. In 1889-90 he followed this with an even more generous gift of 49 acres of land in east Reading. This was to provide a much-needed park and space for sports facilities in a heavily populated part of the town. The land was enclosed in railings and planted with trees at George Palmer's expense.

To acknowledge this gift the delighted public subscribed for the erection of a statue in his honour. The equally delighted Town Council voted to make him the first Honorary Freeman of the Borough.

The statue, which was by George Simonds, showed George Palmer standing in a typical attitude, his right hand holding his hat and umbrella while his left hand grasped the lapel of his coat. It was placed in the middle of Broad Street, looking down King Street and King's Road towards his biscuit factory and the new Palmer Park. The unveiling took place on 4 November 1891. On that day George Palmer received the Freedom of the Borough in the Town Hall, attended the unveiling of the statue, watched a grand procession from Broad Street to Palmer Park, and formally handed over the park to the Mayor and Corporation. The procession, in which all the local trades and societies took part, was nearly two miles long and was generally agreed to be the finest ever seen in Reading. In the evening there was a banquet for George Palmer, fireworks in the park, and free entertainments for the public at the Town Hall and the Royal County Theatre.

In this final part of the 19th century the town's educational facilities were much improved. Before 1870, elementary education had been provided by the British School, established since 1810 in Southampton Street, and by a few parochial schools run by the Church of England. As a result of the Education Act of 1870 the Reading School Board was set up (Alfred Sutton and George Palmer being members), and its preliminary survey showed that there were working class areas with many children where no schools were available. Within five years four new elementary schools — Coley, Katesgrove, Silver Street and

George Palmer's statue on its original site in Broad Street.

Newtown — had been built to provide for these areas. By 1902, when the Board handed over to a new Education Committee, there were 12 Board Schools in addition to 11 Church of England and one Catholic elementary school.

In 1877 the Kendrick Schools, endowed with the small part of John Kendrick's legacy which had been saved for the borough, were opened to provide for children of the middle classes. The boys' school occupied a new building in Queen's Road; the girls were accommodated in Watlington House, a large brick house with a walled garden built in 1688 by a clothier named Samuel Watlington.

Reading Grammar School, which had fallen on bad times and had been closed in the 1860s, was revived and reopened in 1871 in an impressive new building in Erleigh Road, of which Alfred Waterhouse was the architect. The Prince of Wales laid the foundation stone in 1870.

Among the independent schools in the town, the Blue Coat School still flourished and had moved in 1853 to a site in Bath Road. In 1890 a public school for boys was founded by the Society of Friends at

Leighton Park in Shinfield Road. High-class private schools for girls included Wilton House in Parkside Road, and Blenheim House in London Road. The latter was to move in 1905 to Kendrick Road and change its name to The Abbey School.

Further education was available at the Schools of Science and Art. These had begun separately, the Art School in West Street in 1860, and the Science School ten years later in Dr Valpy's old Reading School building in Blagrave Street. The latter had been demolished to make way for the new public library and museum. In 1882 the Schools of Science and Art were combined and housed in a new building in the newly formed Valpy Street. Ten years later they formed part of the new Reading University Extension College, opened under the auspices of Christ Church, Oxford. Increasing numbers of courses and students made extra accommodation necessary. The college expanded into the former Hospitium of Reading Abbey, part of which had miraculously survived at the back of the new Town Hall, and which was drastically restored for the use of the college. This, too, was soon overcrowded, and in 1893 the former St Laurence's Vicarage next door was purchased with financial help from Herbert Sutton, Chairman of the College Council. In 1894 a Department of Agriculture was set up. It was augmented in the following year by the British Dairy Institute, transferred from Aylesbury to Reading and accommodated in a new wing opened in 1896. The Department of Agriculture was to win a high reputation and play an important part in the college's rise to university status.

In 1906 the college moved to a spacious site in London Road presented to it by Alfred Palmer, a son of George Palmer. The site included The Acacias, George Palmer's former home. Under the guidance of its energetic and enthusiastic Principal, Dr W.M. Childs, and with the help of generous endowments and donations, notably from the Palmer family and from Lady Wantage, the University College expanded rapidly. In 1926 it was granted a charter of independence and became the University of Reading.

The Edwardian Age

By the turn of the century Reading was best known to most people living in the county and surrounding areas as a shopping centre. This was a role which it was to develop to the full in the 20th century.

In the latter half of the 19th century shops became more important than the weekly market, which was reduced to a remnant of its former self. Commerce took over the whole of the town centre. Broad Street, Oxford Street, Friar Street, Minster Street, King Street and Market Place were lined with shops. Their business was to satisfy the demands of the growing population for the ever-increasing range of factory-produced goods made so readily available by rail transport.

King Street, looking westwards, at the turn of the century.

House furnishing stores, milliners and outfitters flourished, catering for the elaborately furnished homes and the elaborately dressed people of the Victorian and Edwardian eras. Old-established shops in particular lines of business became household names. Some of the best known were Watson's china shop in Minster Street, Wellsteed's drapery and millinery in Broad Street, Botly & Lewis in King Street and Bracher & Sydenham in Minster Street, both jewellers and silversmiths, Attwell's piano and music warehouse in Friar Street, Stransom's the tailors and outfitters in Market Place, and Jackson's drapery on the corner of King's Road. Innumerable smaller shops, selling practically everything imaginable, ensured that whatever the customer wanted could be got in Reading.

In addition a more comprehensive kind of shop, the department store was beginning to appear. A Reading handbook of 1892 remarked upon the town's 'palatial trading establishments' and referred to that of Messrs Heelas as the largest. This shop had begun in 1854 as a small drapery in Minster Street and had grown 'to the magnitude of the present large and well-conducted emporium'. Heelas' was soon to be rivalled by other fast-growing department stores, notably those of A.H. Bull and William McIlroy. Bull's occupied a major central position on the north side of Broad Street for more than 50 years, during which it expanded through to Friar Street. McIlroy's store was one of the sights of the town when it was opened in 1903. Occupying a prominent corner site in Oxford Street and Cheapside, its huge windows on the ground and first floors, topped by a tall and fantastically ornamented upper storey, easily won for it the nickname of the Crystal Palace.

Other changes to the town's commercial centre were carried out about this time by Councillor J.C. Fidler. A highly successful, self-made businessman, who had begun by building up his father's small fruit shop into the biggest fruit and vegetable shop in town, and the biggest potato warehouse in the country, he had gone on to become a company director with lucrative interests in the City. He also served on the Councils of Reading Borough and of Caversham Urban District. To his energy, initiative and generosity the town owed the rebuilding of the east side of West street, the Market Arcade between Broad Street and Friar Street, the acquisition in 1901 of Prospect Park as a public open space on the western side of Reading, and, finally, Queen Victoria Street.

Councillor Fidler was a farsighted man and, as a Councillor, constantly promoted the idea of the future development of Reading and Caversham as one entity, even proposing to build, at his own expense, a second bridge across the Thames to encourage communication between the two places.

When he died, in December 1903, Queen Victoria Street was nearing completion. This entirely new street was built to provide a much-needed direct way through to Broad Street, the principal shopping street, from the railway stations, at which so many thousands of potential customers arrived. It involved the demolition of various old properties in Broad Street and Friar Street, including Laud Place, some tenements put up in 1813 on the site of Archbishop Laud's birthplace. Queen Victoria Street gave Reading some of its best commercial architecture, the spectacular yellow brick and vermilion terra cotta facades nicely blending ostentation with dignity.

Meanwhile the Great Western Railway Company had been making changes to Reading Station. In 1898-9 the old single platform, used until then by both up and down trains, was replaced by three platforms providing separately for up, down and relief trains, and linked by a 100 yard subway. Passenger facilities were greatly improved by the addition of dining and refreshment rooms. It was remarked that the main station building, a handsome structure in Bath stone put up in the 1860s, now appeared dwarfed by the long and massive platforms and the range of brick buildings on the northern platform.

The area between the station and the town was, at that time, by no means welcoming. As late as 1906 a guidebook described it as 'a sunken meadow given over to stabling and the exercising of horses; beyond, no fine frontage, but only the gaunt backs of ugly houses, and to the left the depressing S.E. station.' The sunken meadow was later filled by industrial and commercial buildings, notably Vincent's motor garage, and Station Road was built up in line with Queen Victoria Street, thus completing a wide thoroughfare leading straight into the commercial heart of Reading.

Within the borough the Corporation began to provide public transport services in 1901, when it took over a private enterprise called the Reading Tramways Company. This had been running horse trams along Oxford Road, Broad Street and King's Road since 1879, its termini being Wilson Road and Cemetery Junction. The tramcars, which by 1901 were in a poor state of repair, and the horses, whose overworked and undernourished condition had been the cause of many complaints from humane persons, did not remain in service much longer. Reading Corporation Tramways, as the new undertaking was called, quickly set about reconstruction and electrification. The existing tramway was extended and new routes laid down with termini in London Road, Erleigh Road, Whitley Street, Bath Road and Caversham Road. A new depot and a power station were built in Mill Lane, on a site occupied for centuries by St Giles' Mill. On 21 July 1903 the horse trams ceased to run.

The opening of the electric tramways on 22 July caused nearly as much excitement, in Reading at least, as the opening of the Great Western Railway more than 60 years earlier. The ceremony was preceded, as was usual in those opulent Edwardian days, by a luncheon for 300 guests in the Large Town Hall, followed by several enthusiastic speeches and toasts. Afterwards, the entire assembly made its way to the Mill Lane depot, where the Mayoress switched on the current and declared the tramways open.

Tramcar no. 1, heavily decked with flags and driven by the Mayor, Alderman A.H. Bull, then led a procession of ten tramcars, all laden with guests, along the Oxford and Wokingham Road routes, and back to Broad Street. The town was crowded with spectators, and, as soon as the Mayor and other distinguished persons had alighted, hundreds of them surged forward, eager to be among the first fare-paying passengers. For several days, cars on all routes were packed until late at

Broad Street, looking eastwards, about 1905.

night, and even then many people were disappointed and had to return home without having had a ride.

The trams were an immense success, being a boon to working people as well as to shoppers coming into the town centre. They served the town well for over 30 years, the last tram being run on 20 May 1939. The first motor buses were introduced on a route between Caversham and Tilehurst in December 1919, and on 21 May 1939 trolleybuses replaced trams on two east-west routes.

In this relatively happy and prosperous period commercial entertainment flourished, both the late Victorians and the Edwardians being fond of lavish and lighthearted shows in luxurious surroundings. It was the age of music hall and musical comedy. The theatre industry was well-organised and, like the manufacturing industries, had reaped enormous benefits from the railways. Theatre proprietors owned chains of theatres, at which frequent changes of programme were made possible by the many railborne touring companies, which brought the latest London successes to the most distant provincial audiences.

Reading, by no means distant from London, enjoyed an excellent choice of plays and shows at the New Royal County Theatre, opened in 1895 on the site of an earlier theatre in Friar Street. This theatre, designed by a leading theatre architect, Frank Matcham, was typical of the period. It was luxurious, glamorous and a little exotic. Theatregoers were drawn into its world of fantasy through a vestibule in which vivid green palms and ferns stood reflected in huge mirrors, and rose-coloured lamps glowed from a richly carved ceiling. The auditorium welcomed them with velvet-covered seats, warm leather wallpaper and elaborately draped plush curtains around the proscenium and boxes.

Here were presented all the hit musicals of the time — *The Arcadians, The Merry Widow, The Quaker Girl, The Chocolate Soldier* — and dramas such as *Trilby, The Sign of the Cross, The Silver King* and *The Speckled Band.*

In 1907 another theatre, The Palace, was opened in Cheapside. It was built by a group of local businessmen who believed that the demand for variety entertainment in Reading was sufficient to make a second theatre a profitable investment. The Palace was designed by W.G.R. Sprague, who had designed several famous London theatres. Its interior, compared with that of the Royal County Theatre, was elegant and simple. It was decorated in the Adam style and painted in delicate shades of cream and terra-cotta, outlined with gold.

Owing to the number of serious theatre fires which had taken place all over the country, the Palace was constructed almost entirely of steel and concrete, and every part of the building was designed with the safety of audience, staff and performers in mind. A memorable feature was the seating in 'the gods' which was in the form of concrete steps, thinly carpeted.

The Palace did well as a variety theatre for many years, George Robey, Harry Tate, Marie Lloyd and Florrie Forde being among the host of famous performers who appeared there. It survived the Royal County Theatre, destroyed by fire in 1937, by more than twenty years, and was knocked down by a demolition gang in 1961.

The Edwardians were the first to enjoy motion pictures. The year 1909 saw the opening of Reading's first three cinemas — Bio-Picture Land in King's Road, the Vaudeville Electric in Broad Street, and West's Picture Palace in West Street. Two years later the Grand Cinema was opened in Broad Street, and the Glendale in Caversham.

Of these, the Vaudeville was to be the most successful, although West's tried hard at first and attracted audiences with novelty competitions and mechanical sound effects to accompany the events shown on the screen. In December 1909 its proprietor advertised it as 'An ideal place to spend a happy Christmas. Warm, comfortable and luxuriously appointed. A splendid programme for the holidays, unique, refined and irresistably amusing. Accompanied by a magnificent Orchestra and Full Mechanical Effects.'

West's and Bio-Picture Land were closed in World War I, and the Grand closed in 1922. The Vaudeville survived and, in 1921, was rebuilt in a far more splendid style, with a marvellous decor which earned it the title of Reading's Temple of Colour and Harmony.

The Boundary Extension of 1911

In 1911 the boundaries of Reading were again extended, and the area of the borough increased to 9,106 acres. In this extension the new territory included nearly the whole of Caversham and Tilehurst.

Caversham, many of whose 9,800 inhabitants strongly objected to the merger, was a large village which had become a fashionable residential suburb of Reading. Until 1911 it had been wholly in Oxfordshire, and the barrier of the Thames had enabled it to lead an existence separate from that of its much larger and busier neighbour. In the late 19th century many new streets had been added to the village, and since 1891 Caversham had been governed by its own Urban District Council.

The original parish church of St Peter was founded in Norman times, but the surviving building was mostly the result of 19th century restoration. There were several other modern churches of various persuasions. Queen Anne's School for girls, run by the Grey Coat Foundation of London, had been established there since 1894. The village had also five elementary schools, a free public library, a cinema, and a police station manned by an inspector, a sergeant and six constables.

The principal landowner and lord of the manor was W.T. Crawshay, Esq., of Caversham Park. The Crawshay family had made its fortune from the great Cyfarthfa ironworks in South Wales during the first half of the 19th century, and Caversham Park had been purchased in a state of decay by Crawshay's grandfather, who had rebuilt it in grand style, adding imposing colonnaded wings.

Other notable houses sharing the hillside with Caversham Park were Caversham Grove, Caversham Hill and Balmore. Close by St Peter's Church stood Caversham Rectory, later known as Caversham Court, parts of which dated back to the 17th century. Its beautiful terraced gardens still overlook the river, although the house has been demolished. Almost a mile away downstream was Caversham Mill,

146

and, near it, the cluster of small Victorian streets which made up Lower Caversham. New Caversham was developing on the wooded slopes above St Peter's Church, where terraced houses as well as more exclusive properties were being built.

Tilehurst, although an extensive parish, was more rural, its population amounting to little more than 3,000. It was situated mostly on high ground, and contained several farms. Brickmaking was an old-established local industry. The village, gathered around St Michael's Church, was three miles from the centre of Reading, and the roads to it ran uphill nearly all the way. Traditionally, transport into Reading was by carrier's cart (two carriers ran daily services), but since 1903 the borough tramway along Oxford Road had brought this means of conveyance to within a mile of the village.

The principal landowner and lord of the manor was Henry Barry Blagrave, Esq., of Calcot Park. The Blagrave family had formerly shown a keen interest in village affairs. Henry Barry's father had contributed generously towards the cost of the village hall, opened in 1894. His mother had arranged regular treats and outings for the

School Road, Tilehurst, at the beginning of the 20th century.

children of Calcot Infants' School in Calcot Row. The Blagrave recreation ground, opened in 1896, occupied land given for the purpose. Henry Barry Blagrave, however, was rarely at Calcot. A great traveller, sportsman and big game hunter, he spent much of his life abroad.

Tilehurst village had had a school since the National School was founded in 1819. This was replaced by Norcot School in 1906. Grovelands School, opened in 1880, had been taken into the borough of Reading in the extension of 1887, and Park Lane School had been built to replace it.

In recent years, Tilehurst had begun to develop as a residential area, particularly in the direction of its railway station, opened in 1882 beside the Oxford Road. Many new houses and small shops were being built on the north side of the village.

When Reading was granted its boundary extension in 1911, the Extension Order stipulated that the existing bridge over the Thames must be rebuilt or widened to 45 feet at least, to provide an effective means of communication between Caversham and the rest of the borough. In addition, a footbridge at least ten feet wide was to be built linking Lower Caversham with Reading.

The Corporation's plans to carry out these works were frustrated by the outbreak of World War I.

World War I and After

In World War I the whole nation was, for the first time, involved in a war effort. In Reading, as elsewhere, the lives of the people were disrupted in many ways. In March 1915 the military authorities took over the borough workhouse and infirmary in Oxford Road (renamed Battle Infirmary after the war) and converted it into the Reading War Hospital. Here, thousands of sick and wounded men were brought from the battlefields for care and treatment. Extra hospital accommodation was found by taking over several local schools, including Redlands, Battle and Wilson Schools. The Royal Berkshire Hospital also provided beds for hundreds of wounded men. Large country houses in the area, such as Englefield and Basildon, were given by their owners for use as convalescent homes. Reading Station was constantly busy with the arrival and departure of trainloads of soldiers, and the Voluntary Aid Transport services, organised by the Berkshire Automobile Club, were fully occupied running ambulances between the station and the various hospitals and convalescent homes.

Another voluntary organisation, called the Friends of the Wounded, set up and ran, from 1915 to the end of the war, the Reading War Hospitals Supplies Depot, based in Duke Street. The Friends made surgical necessities for war hospitals abroad as well as in England, and produced large quantities of swabs, bandages, padded splints and crutches, as well as special items such as pneumonia jackets, mosquito nets and pieces of orthopaedic equipment for individual patients. Further contributions were made by the children of various schools, the girls' schools producing sewn articles and the boys' schools metal and woodwork appliances.

As the war progressed the town's population was swollen by the influx of families from London, creating housing problems and overcrowding in the schools, already acutely short of space owing to the requirements of the War Hospital. Local industries suffered because of the shortage of raw materials and the loss of men to the armed forces. Many factories went over to war work. At Huntley & Palmers the engineering department made shells and machined parts for aircraft engines and apparatus for gun rifling. The firm's railway system was used as a marshalling yard for munitions made in Reading.

The enormous casualties of the war brought tragedy to thousands of local families; week after week the Reading newspapers carried photographs and stories of men killed, wounded, missing or prisoners of war.

After the war Reading took time to recover, but it was fortunate in that, during the national economic depression of the 1920s and 30s, it did not suffer so badly as many other towns, particularly those in the north of England, which were dependent upon one industry. In Reading, the number and variety of industries and occupations meant that there was at no time any large-scale unemployment.

In politics, however, the Labour movement gained favour. Before the war, the only Labour candidate to stand for Reading had been Harry Quelch in 1898. As the first challenger to the local Liberals and Conservatives he polled only 270 votes. In 1923 Reading elected its first Labour M.P., Dr Somerville Hastings, with over 16,000 votes. He was defeated by the Conservative candidate in 1924, but returned again at the General Election of 1929. The almost equal division of political opinion was reflected in Reading's attitude to the General Strike in 1926, when most of the town's factories remained at work, and it was left to the tram drivers and printers to strike in sympathy with the miners and railway men.

Although the war and its aftermath caused a slowing-down of the rapid development of the town which had marked the late 19th and early 20th centuries, Reading continued to make progress. Its first major achievement after the war was the construction of two new bridges over the Thames.

The first to be built was Reading Bridge. It had become clear by the 1920s that more than one bridge would be needed to carry the traffic of the future, and a wide, single-span road bridge was built instead of the proposed footbridge between Lower Caversham and Reading. Reading Bridge was completed in 1923, and, its strength having been tested by a spectacular procession of steam rollers, it was officially opened on 23 October that year.

In 1924-26 the unsatisfactory iron bridge put up in 1868-9 was replaced by a sturdy bridge of ferro-concrete, spanning the Thames

Steam rollers testing the new Reading Bridge in 1923.

with two long, low arches. The new Caversham Bridge was finished in time for a planned official opening by the Prince of Wales in May 1926, but the General Strike prevented this. The Prince came on 25 June to unveil a commemorative plaque on the bridge, and to visit other parts of the town.

The completion of the bridges made further improvements to the river banks necessary. Thames Side Promenade, on the Reading side of the river, had been laid out in 1907. Now, the Caversham bank between the bridges was laid out with formal walks, and playing fields for children were provided.

The Corporation's next major achievement was the new Kendrick Girls' School. After years of negotiation with the Board of Education, the town's foremost grammar school for girls was able to move out of its cramped quarters in Watlington House. Kendrick School was built on a corner site in Sidmouth Street and London Road, and was opened in 1927.

House building, to ease the serious housing shortage, occupied the Council throughout the inter-war years, and the built-up area of the town began to grow again as new estates were developed. The first council housing estate, in Shinfield Road,was begun in 1920. A proposed estate of 350 houses at Norcot had to be shelved because of financial restraints imposed by central government, but in 1931 work began on a large estate at Whitley. At the same time, condemned properties in the poorest parts of the town, notably Coley, were demolished. In the late 1930s private housing estates were built at Kentwood in Tilehurst, and in Henley Road, Caversham, and Berkeley Avenue, Reading.

The increasing volume of traffic made a number of road widenings and improvements necessary. In Broad Street, traffic jams in the 1920s caused the removal of George Palmer's statue, put up in 1891. It was re-erected in Palmer Park in 1930.

On the outskirts of the borough, signs of the old order passing away were to be seen in the breaking-up of family estates and the decay of large country houses.

The first to go was Southcote Manor House, an early home of the Blagrave family. A house had stood on this Kennet valley site since the 13th century; a moat, drawbridge and 15th century watch tower survived as reminders of its antiquity. The house itself had been rebuilt and restored several times. It was surrounded within the moat by terraced gardens, and, across the bridge, stood a large block of stabling. Since the beginning of the century the property had been allowed to decay, and when, in 1918, it was put up for sale it found no buyer. In 1921 all the buildings inside the moat were demolished. The derelict garden, stables and partly filled-in moat remained until the site was cleared for a council housing estate in the 1960s.

The owner of Southcote was H.B. Blagrave of Calcot Park. In 1918 he had put up for sale the outlying parts of the Calcot estate, including Southcote Manor and Lodge, Calcot Place, and ten farms of which Beansheaf, Langley, Pincent's and Turnham's Farms occupied almost the whole area of south-west Tilehurst. In 1919 and again in 1926 Calcot Park itself was put up for auction, but found no buyer on either occasion. Henry Barry Blagrave died in 1927, leaving no heir. Two years later a group of local gentlemen raised enough money for the purchase of the property and its conversion into a golf course, retaining Calcot Park House as the club house.

In Earley, two historic estates lying close to the borough boundary came up for sale in the 1930s. Maiden Erlegh, situated between Wokingham Road, Wilderness Road, Beech Lane and Mill Lane, had belonged since 1903 to Solomon Barnato Joel, the multi-millionaire and racehorse owner. During his ownership the mansion, which had been built in the late 19th century on the site of an earlier house, was greatly improved. Luxurious additions included a palm court, a magnificent marble indoor swimming pool with veined marble pillars on either side of the pool, beautiful ornamental gardens, a stud farm and sports grounds for croquet, cricket, tennis and bowls. Solly Joel's Sunday-before-Ascot luncheons were famous. In 1927 the Duke of York (later George VI) lunched at Maiden Erlegh when he came to open the Solly Joel Playing Field in Reading.

Solly Joel died in 1931. The estate was sold in 1932 and s the contents of the house were auctioned. Maiden Erlegh School was next established there until 1942, when it was again sold. After several chequered years, in which it was used, among other purposes, as offices for Imperial Chemical Industries Ltd., and accommodation for Hungarian refugees, the estate was finally sold for building developments and the house was demolished in 1960.

Little more than a month after the sale of Maiden Erlegh in 1932, the Erleigh Court estate was sold. This lay along the London Road with Culver Lane and Pitts Lane as its southern boundary, and was once the mediaeval manor of Erlegh St Bartholomew. The house was of mixed periods, part 16th and part 18th century. In the 19th century it had belonged to Lord Stowell, in whose time an ancient farmhouse on the estate had been converted into a residence called Sidmouth Grange. After Lord Stowell's death in 1836 the estate passed to his daughter and son-in-law, Lord and Lady Sidmouth. The Sidmouth's not only gave the site for the Royal Berkshire Hospital in Reading, but the site and a generous endowment for the parish church of St Peter, in Earley, opened in 1844. The Erleigh Court estate remained in the Sidmouth family until 1932, when it was sold for building development. The house was demolished in 1935.

In south Reading, Coley Park estate, between the Kennet and Bath Road, had belonged throughout the 19th century to the Monck family, who had served Reading well as M.P.s, Town Councillors and Justices of the Peace. After the death in 1905 of William Berkeley Monck, the family moved away, the contents of the house being sold and the house let. In 1937 the estate was put up for auction. Being so close to the town it already contained a large number of rented properties, and had been badly cut up by railway lines. Since World War II Coley Park House has been occupied by the Ministry of Agriculture and a block of modern offices has been built beside it.

At Caversham, W.T. Crawshay had died without an heir in 1918, and his widow in 1920. Caversham Park stood empty for two years until it was acquired by the Catholic Oratory School, transferred from Birmingham. In 1926 the house was seriously damaged by fire, but the school remained there until the early 1940s. After the school moved out of Reading Caversham Park was taken over in 1942 by the B.B.C., and the overseas monitoring station was established there.

One exciting and hopeful new development on the outskirts of the borough in the 1930s was Reading Aerodrome. This owed its existence to Charles Powis, partner in the firm of Phillips & Powis, which made pedal and motor cycles in Reading. In 1928, fired with enthusiasm after a flight to Paris, Charles Powis bought 130 acres of land in Woodley and created an airfield there. A small hangar and repaid shop were built, and a flying school started which later became the Reading Aero Club. At the opening of the Club in May 1931 Amy Johnson came to Woodley to take part in an air-race for light planes. Crowds of spectators came from Reading and elsewhere to see her, as they did for many other air displays at Woodley in the 1930s. The facilities of the

Mr and Mrs F. G. Miles with test pilot John Lawn (left) and the Kestrel trainer, prototype of the Miles Master, at Woodley Aerodrome in 1937.

new Aerodrome were used by sporting and professional flyers from other parts of the country. It was here in 1931 that the 21-year-old pilot Douglas Bader, visiting Woodley with an RAF aerobatics team, crashed, injuring his legs so badly that both had to be amputated.

Meanwhile, Phillips & Powis, working in cramped and primitive conditions, had begun to produce light aircraft. In 1932 they were joined by aircraft designer F.G. Miles, who was keen to develop a new kind of monoplane. The result was the Miles Hawk, which took to the air in 1933 and was an instant success. Phillips & Powis then went into full production of the Hawk and subsequent models. By 1936 they were making 14 different types of plane and were one of the country's leading manufacturers of light civilian aircraft. Miles aircraft could be seen at aerodromes all over Britain and in many other countries. They took part in the great air racing events of the period, including the England to Australia Race in 1934, and the England to Johannesburg Jubilee Race in 1936. Thirteen Miles aircraft took part in the Kings Cup Race in 1935. It was won by the firm's New Falcon, flown by Flight Lieutenant Tommy Rose, the famous World War I pilot.

Reading in the Second World War

At the outbreak of World War II Reading was regarded by the Government as sufficiently far from London to be designated a 'safe town' in the event of aerial bombing. Many of the inhabitants did not share this view. Some thought that its railway junction alone would make it a target for enemy attack, while others feared that Reading, like all towns in the south-east, would be razed to the ground by German bombers. In the event, official opinion turned out to be correct. Reading suffered only one air raid in the whole course of the war.

As a safe town it was used as a reception town for evacuees and refugees from London and the south-east. About 25,000 of these were brought here under official schemes, billets being found for them and billeting allowances paid, but thousands more came unofficially and fended for themselves. In addition, a number of firms and offices, including some Government offices, were transferred to Reading, bringing hundreds of employees with them. Nearly 9,000 householders received billeting notices under official schemes; many others took in evacuees and refugees under private and voluntary arrangements.

Reading's major wartime problem, therefore, was overcrowding. In 1939 its population was about 100,000. In 1942 it was nearly 140,000, and, since October of the previous year, accommodation had been so scarce that Reading had been declared a 'closed town'. The local council was given authority to control the influx of new inhabitants; the consent of the Billeting Officer had to be obtained before any person could take up residence, and he had to be notified when any person moved away.

Little could be done to ease the housing problem. The shortage of materials meant that all housebuilding ceased in 1940, and for the rest of the war Government controls ensured that licences were only issued for top priority work or for essential repairs to war damaged buildings.

The school population of the town was increased by about 55 per cent, placing an almost intolerable burden on the 44 schools which

156

were already coping with over 13,000 children. At the start of the war, all kinds of improvisations were necessary to accommodate the sudden, large influx of newcomers, and to ensure that all the children, whether local or evacuated, received a little education, however disrupted. Some evacuated schools were accommodated in church halls or any other large building which happened to be available. Others shared local schools on a double shift basis. It was not only the children who had to share. At Battle School, at one time during the emergency, there were three local head teachers and ten evacuated head teachers.

The situation grew easier as the accommodation problems were sorted out and supplementary buildings made available, sometimes in the form of pre-fabricated huts. By 1942, when the intensity of air attacks on the south-east had diminished, the numbers of children decreased as evacuated families began to drift back to their homes.

As the war had been long anticipated, central and local government contingency plans had been formed well in advance. In Reading, the Borough Council prepared and published its Air Raid Precautions Scheme as early as 1937. While repeating the official opinion that Reading, from a military point of view, was not of strategic importance, and that a large scale planned raid was unlikely, the Council pointed out that there would be the danger of isolated attacks. The Air Raid Precautions Scheme described the voluntary organisations of men and women which would be needed to keep watch over Reading and deal with any emergencies. These included auxiliary fire services, rescue services, air raid warden services, first aid parties, road and public utility repair parties, and decontamination squads in the event of attack with poisonous gas. The public were also given instructions in advance concerning air raid warnings, the distribution of gas masks, and black-out precautions.

By the time war broke out, Reading's Civil Defence was well organised and the Civil Defence Emergency Committee was able to issue a complete list of names and addresses of air raid wardens, wardens posts (there were 64 in the borough, each equipped with a blast-proof telephone) ambulance depots, auxiliary fire stations, rescue and repair parties. Anderson shelters were being delivered for erection in the gardens of many homes, and about 40 public air raid shelters had been prepared in the town centre, mostly in shop basements and subways. In addition, trenches had been dug for shelter in Palmer Park and at Coley.

The Women's Voluntary Services for Civil Defence had been formed in response to an appeal from the Home Secretary in 1938, the Chairman of the national organisation being the Dowager Marchioness of Reading. Right at the start of the war the W.V.S. in Reading played a vital part in the reception of the thousands of evacuees arriving at Reading, providing billeting escorts, transport and other assistance.

In 1940, after the fall of France, the threat of invasion was very real and the Local Defence Volunteers, later called the Home Guard, began training in earnest. Many of them were men aged between 50 and 60. They had, at first, no uniforms and were ill-armed with old rifles, swords and even clubs. Within a few months they were uniformed, armed with modern weapons and trained in street fighting and marksmanship. Groups of them were taken to the Berkshire Downs to practice manoeuvres.

The Home Guard kept special watch over sites which, it was believed, would be the enemy's main targets in the event of an attack. These included the river bridges, the railway marshalling yards, Brock Barracks, the Town Hall, gas and electricity works, and large factories such as Sigmund Pulsometer Pumps and Huntley & Palmers. At the Town Hall, sandbags were piled up round the building and armed men stood outside with fixed bayonets. The Reading Borough Charters and other vital documents had been packed into sealed dustbins and sent for storage to some chalk caves near Peppard Road. The thousands of men and women who answered the call to join the emergency defence services faithfully carried out their duties throughout the war. For most of the time these duties were tedious and undramatic, but the men of the Home Guard who manned a rocket battery on the southern outskirts of the town were in action several times and, in addition to the one serious raid, there were six other occasions when bombs were dropped on various parts of Reading and Caversham. In these minor incidents, which took place in 1940 and 1941, a number of houses and other buildings were badly damaged, three people were slightly injured and a milk roundsman's horse was killed in Berkeley Avenue.

Reading experienced its worst raid of the war on 10 February 1943. On that dull, drizzly day a solitary German bomber (identified by members of the Reading Spotters' Club as a Dornier DO 217) was seen approaching the town. It was flying very low and there was little time in which warning could be given. The aircraft made a short, terrifying run across the town, dropping a stick of bombs and machine-gunning people in the streets of north Reading and Caversham.

The four bombs fell in a line extending from Minster Street to Friar Street. The back of Wellsteed's (now Debenhams's) store was completely wrecked, and so was the northern half of the covered Market Arcade. St Laurence's Church lost nearly all its stained glass and the pinnacles on its tower were rendered so unsafe that they had later to be removed. The front of Blandy & Blandy's offices was blown away and the Town Clerk's offices in the adjoining Town Hall were badly damaged. Fortunately it was a Wednesday afternoon and the shops were closed, but a restaurant called the People's Pantry at the Friar Street end of the Arcade was crowded, and it was there that most of the casualties occurred. When the Civil Defence workers had completed their task it was found that 41 people had been killed, 49 seriously injured and 104 slightly injured.

Reading's factories contributed to the war effort in the production of munitions and in various branches of engineering. An important contribution was made by the Phillips & Powis aircraft factory at Woodley. In 1935 the firm's Miles Hawk Trainer had been approved by the Air Ministry for the training of Air Force personnel, and a Royal Air Force Civil Training School was established at Reading

Bomb damage to the Town Hall, Blandy & Blandy's offices and St Laurence's Church, caused by the air raid on 10 February 1943.

Aerodrome. Three years later, when the long expected war was imminent and the Government had approved the expansion of the Air Force, the new kinds of fighters and bombers then being produced made a new kind of training aircraft necessary, and a large contract was awarded to Phillips & Powis to build the Miles Magister, a military version of the Hawk Trainer.

The size of the contract necessitated considerable additions to the factory and huge new buildings went up on Woodley airfield. Woodley itself began to grow as the demand for a larger work force brought more people to the area, for whom houses, shops and other amenities had to be provided. In 1939 Sir Kingsley Wood, the Air Minister, came to open a new factory set up to build the Miles Master, a high-speed training aircraft designed to match the new Hurricane and Spitfire. The result was a boom in the aircraft industry at Woodley. The firm which, between 1929 and 1937, built 354 aircraft, built more than 5,000 between 1938 and 1945. In addition, 3,000 other planes which had been damaged in action were repaired or rebuilt, and these included Spitfires, Oxfords and other types not made at Woodley. In 1943 the firm was renamed Miles Aircraft Ltd. after its famous designer. At its peak period of wartime activity it employed over 7,000 workers.

The town of Reading also contributed to the war effort by accommodating a variety of Government departments evacuated from London. Large houses standing empty and any other available buildings were taken over for the purpose, and Reading became a regional administrative centre.

Early in the war Caversham Park, which had been unoccupied for some time, became the home of the B.B.C.'s Monitoring Service. This service had begun in August 1939, when the B.B.C. and the then embryo Ministry of Information had set up a listening unit to intercept, record and translate broadcasts from enemy and neutral countries. Throughout the war the Monitoring Service played a vital role as 'the ears of Britain', collecting and transmitting essential information to the Government, its Ministers and to the B.B.C. for its news bulletins. Many of the monitors were refugees listening to the news, all too often tragic, from their own countries. By the end of the war the service had developed into the largest and most efficient listening post in the world, monitoring more than a million words a day in 30 languages.

It was at Caversham Park that the first news of the capitulation of Germany was received in May 1945.

Reading Today

After the war came several years of austerity, when shortages of building materials, fuel and other essential supplies inhibited progress and had the effect of preserving the town in its pre-war state. But it was all a great deal dingier and shabbier. Buildings were in a poor state of repair and sadly in need of fresh paint. Road surfaces were in such bad condition that there were frequent complaints concerning the dangers of getting about the town, particularly after dark. Some of the main thoroughfares were still partly cobbled and rutted with long-disused tramlines, and the network of lines at Cemetery Junction was notorious. Numerous potholes created additional hazards for workers, hundreds of whom travelled to and from work on bicycles through poorly lighted streets. Although most of the damage caused by the air raid in 1943 was repaired soon after the war, the derelict Market Arcade remained boarded up until well into the 1950s, and was often condemned in the local press as 'an eyesore' and 'an ugly scar on the face of the town'.

The shortage of fuel was most acutely felt in the first bitter months of 1947, when a prolonged spell of snow and frost caused a national fuel crisis. Electricity supplies were reduced, street lights put out, working hours staggered, and the precious contents of domestic coal sheds eked out to the last lump and shovelful of dust. At last, in March, came the thaw, but with it, in the Thames Valley, came the worst floods for more than 50 years. Caversham was one of the worst affected areas. During the night of Friday, 14 March, the Thames rose 15 inches, and householders in Lower Caversham going downstairs on Saturday morning were astonished to find that the river had taken possession of their ground floors.

Twenty streets including some 1600 houses were affected. Caversham Road and Vastern Road were both flooded under the railway bridges, making communication with Reading difficult. A state of emergency was immediately declared and a ferry service with punts, dinghies and high-wheeled lorries was improvised. On the following Tuesday these conveyances were joined by two amphibious 'ducks' loaned by the War Office.

It was a week before the floods subsided and many more weeks before the householders were back to normal, but during the emergency the Police, the Women's Voluntary Services, the Thames watermen and the people themselves rose magnificently to the occasion. More than 200 families had to be evacuated and provided with temporary accommodation. The W.V.S. worked long hours delivering food and providing meals for people marooned in their homes, and the School Meals Service laid on hot mid-day meals at the former British Restaurant in King's Road. The Mayor, Ald. Mrs Phoebe Cusden, was out by dawn each day helping to serve hot drinks.

Soap, coal and bread were delivered by the Police, in some cases by means of buckets lowered from top-floor windows. The floods were so deep that householders lucky enough to have some coal could not get at it under the water, while those who had supplies of coke could only watch helplessly as their fuel floated away downstream.

For a few days Reading was front-page news in the national press, and the Thames Conservancy issued daily statements concerning the flood situation. The Conservancy reported that an even worse disaster had been narrowly averted at Caversham lock, where, but for the prompt action taken by the Divisional Engineer, the lock itself would have been washed away. The Flood Distress Fund opened by the Mayor reached nearly £12,000 by the end of May, including a generous grant of £5,000 from the Lord Mayor of London's Fund.

Six years later, when the Queen's coronation in 1953 heralded the beginning of what was called the New Elizabethan Age, the aftermath of war was still to be seen and felt. The *Reading Standard* for 2 January that year commented, "In the New Year upon which we have just entered, the British people are once again called upon to produce more and spend less. For near a decade this austere bidding has been heard, and people may be forgiven if they are weary of it, if they are sceptical of ever seeing an end to austerity." Government controls and restrictions still affected most aspects of everyday life. Foods such as meat, butter, cheese and sugar were still rationed; others were in short supply. Tea had been de-rationed only since the previous autumn.

Early in the year the Coronation Celebrations Committee met to discuss what could be done, on a small budget, to mark the event. The Borough Architect put forward a scheme for the decoration of public and municipal buildings, proposing flags and flowers in the main streets, floodlighting of the Forbury Gardens, the Town Hall

The Thames in flood at Reading and Caversham, March 1947.

clocktower, St Laurence's Church and St Mary's Church; and fairy lamps in the Forbury Gardens and Christchurch Playing Fields and along Thames Side Promenade. The Committee decided that the programme of events for Coronation Day should include band concerts, athletics, water sports, dancing, a fun fair in Hill's Meadow, a procession, and fireworks. The Mayor, Councillor Frank Lewis, would plant a tree in the Forbury Gardens after a civic service at St Laurence's Church on the Sunday preceding the Coronation, and during the festivities the borough would entertain a delegation from Reading, Pennsylvania, thus returning hospitality shown to previous Mayors of Reading during visits to the United States.

Meanwhile the Reading Chamber of Commerce was urging its members to brighten up the town with fresh paint, and to clear away rubbish from untidy corners. A Cleaner Shop Windows Campaign was suggested, because the work of window dressers was spoilt by dirty windows. One member lamented the gleaming shop windows of pre-war days and remarked that shop staff could no longer be asked to clean a window without provoking a riot. "I remember", he said, "when shop assistants would run out and polish off a mark as soon as it was made, but that is not done in these days."

By the middle of May the town had been transformed and people were looking forward to the Coronation festivities. The streets were hung with red, white and blue flags and flowers, and blazoned with royal crowns and coats of arms. The shops were full of souvenir mugs, teapots, trays, tablemeats, money-boxes and picture books. Smith's (Reading) Coaches were kept busy running daily trips to London to see the magnificent decorations along the Coronation route, and television dealers coped frantically with last-minute demands for sets to be installed before the great day. The prospect of watching the Coronation on television had led to a tremendous boom in sales and it was estimated that the number of television owners in Reading rose to more than 7,000. In 1946, when Reading issued its first TV licences, they had numbered only 46.

On the morning of 2 June the streets were quiet and a *Reading Standard* reporter wrote, "For most of Coronation Day Reading might have been an almost deserted town. A cold north wind swept through the empty streets, raising a swirling dust and setting flags and bunting fluttering on their fastenings. A few news vendors offered the latest coronation news but, otherwise, there was little to indicate that the country was celebrating the start of a new Elizabethan era. Drawn curtains in house after house and street after street supplied the answer — television, that modern miracle which brought millions of her subjects closer to the Queen during her coronation than many of those who were present in the Abbey."

In the afternoon and early evening the programme of concerts, sports, processions and other events prepared by local organisations was carried out fairly successfully, but cutting winds and chilling temperatures drove many spectators away, and there was much sympathy for the competitors who bravely took part in the water sports. The weather, however, did not dampen the spirits of the people who had arranged their own outdoor parties in the side-streets of Reading. The *Standard* described these as "Spartan festivals with flags flying", and said that these small communities, with spontaneous feeling and rare ingenuity, had made the streets they lived in glow with colour and resound with festive jollity. Tables were laid out of doors and people of all ages sat happily spooning trifles and munching sticky cakes, while the cold wind flapped the table cloths and drizzling rain rapidly cooled their tea.

Late in the evening rain began to fall heavily, and open air dancing due to take place on Thames Side Promenade had to be cancelled. But thousands made their way to Hill's Meadow to watch a firework display and the lighting of a huge bonfire. At the same time, boy scouts were lighting beacons at four high points around the town — Anderson Avenue, Cressingham Road, Cockney Hill and Caversham Heights — and these were links in a countrywide chain of fires lit that night to celebrate the crowning of the Queen.

The new reign saw the beginnings of that process of change and development in Reading which was to accelerate so rapidly and devastatingly that residents cried out for a halt and people who had been away from the town for a few years complained that they could no longer recognise it.

By 1950 building controls had been eased sufficiently to allow the borough council to commence major re-housing projects. The end of the war had found the town seriously overcrowded, and a survey revealed that there were 3,750 families in Reading without homes of their own, and many others whose homes were little better than slums. House building, was given priority, and for this reason the first big changes in Reading after the war were to be seen on the outskirts of the town, where housing estates began to sprawl across the empty land.

The council's first major project was the 150 acre Southcote estate along the Bath Road, which was begun in 1950. Families began to move in two years later. Next, roads and sewers were laid down between Reading and Tilehurst in preparation for another large housing development, causing country lovers to protest against the loss of amenities. They protested in vain. Fields, copses and footpaths disappeared under the St Michael's estate and the new concrete Meadway. In south Reading the Whitley estate, begun before the war, was extended southwards to Whitley Wood. Another council estate was built in Caversham at Emmer Green.

These, and other developments, soon resulted in a land shortage which caused the council to revise its policy with regard to high-rise buildings. There had been some opposition to these, although a few enthusiasts argued that 'finding space in the sky' would solve all the planning problems of the future. As a result, the first eight-storey council flats were built at Southcote and occupied in 1959. A year later two 15-storey blocks went up at Coley.

Beyond Reading's eastern boundary Earley and Woodley were growing fast as residential areas. In Earley, more houses were built on the land formerly belonging to the Erleigh Court and Maiden Erlegh estates, where developments had been started before the war. An important event affecting this area took place in 1947, when the whole of the Whiteknights Park estate was acquired for the University of Reading. The University had long outgrown its London Road site, and Government plans to extend university education after the war had created an urgent need for space in which to expand. The first new buildings began to go up in the park in 1954, and, gradually, most of the university departments were transferred to Whiteknights.

Lower Earley, bounded by the M4 and the River Loddon, was to become, in the 1970s, the subject of a huge new development plan designed to provide 8-9,000 houses for up to 20,000 people.

Woodley, before the war, was a mainly rural parish in which the Bulmershe estate occupied most of the western half, while the eastern half contained a number of scattered hamlets and the Reading aerodrome. After the war Woodley developed as a dormitory suburb of Reading, although separate from it and administered as part of Wokingham District. It has its own schools, churches, shopping precincts and other amenities, and in 1974, when its population was approaching 29,000 it was granted town status.

In spite of the initial success of the aerodrome and the high reputation won by Miles' Aircraft before and during the war, the aircraft factory failed to win contracts after the war and was overcome by financial difficulties in 1947. By that time it had been reduced to making a number of minor products such as ball-point pens and photocopying machines. Its aircraft assets were taken over by Handley Page Ltd., who continued to make aircraft there until 1962. After that, plane making ceased at Woodley. The airfield site was purchased by Adwest Properties Ltd., and plots were leased out to various manufacturing and light engineering firms, including Huntley, Boorne & Stevens, the tin-box maskers who grew up with Huntley & Palmers' and who moved to Woodley from their cramped premises in London Street in 1969.

Woodley Lodge, in its later years called Bulmershe Court, was demolished in 1963 and the Berkshire College of Education was built upon its site.

In the last 30 years commerce has drastically changed the face of central Reading. At the start of the 1950s the main shopping centre was much the same as it had been at the outbreak of war, and changes were only just beginning to take place. Most of the old familiar shops, such as Baylis the grocers, Hill's leather goods, Archer's hardware and

Colebrook's the butchers, were still trading in Broad Street. These, and many others, were soon to disappear, as were the Cadena Café and Lyons' teashop. The old Vaudeville Cinema, opened in 1909 and renamed Gaumont in 1953, survived on the north side of Broad Street until 1957, when it was demolished to make way for Timothy White's (now Boot's). Where the British Home Stores now stands was the Angel public house, once one of Reading's busiest coaching inns. On the opposite side of Broad Street a modest Marks & Spencer's showed no sign of its later expansion through to Cross Street and Friar Street.

The four principal department stores were still Wellsteed's, Bull's, Heelas and McIlroy's. Of these, Bull's was to close in 1953, and McIlroy's two years later. Heelas, already taken over by United Drapery in 1949, was taken over by the John Lewis Partnership in 1953. Wellsteed's eventually became Debenham's.

Commercial developments in the shape of supermarkets and pedestrian precincts changed the style of shopping in Reading as in other towns. Many small food shops were ousted by supermarkets, among the first of which in central Reading was Sainsbury's, opened in Friar Street in 1963. At the corner of St Mary's Butts and Oxford Street a huge area was cleared of an assortment of old shops and houses and redeveloped as the Butts Centre, a spacious, undercover, air-conditioned shopping complex with its own roof-top car park, opened in 1972. On the north side of Friar Street another large shopping precinct named Friar's Walk was opened in 1973-4. The Victorian Market Arcade, built by Councillor Fidler in the 1890s and badly damaged during the war, was demolished and a modern arcade was built in sections between 1957 and 1965, linking Broad Street, Friar Street and Market Place.

In the course of modernisation many decorative and distinctive old buildings were torn down and replaced by featureless and often ugly new ones. Within a few years public protest against the destruction of old Reading led to the formation, in 1961, of the Reading Civic Society. As a result several threatened buildings were saved. A plan, which had been partly carried out, to redevelop the entire Market Place on modern lines was halted, and subsequent practice favoured the preservation of the facades of old buildings while providing interiors designed to suit twentieth-century needs.

In 1970 shopping in Broad Street was made more enjoyable by the exclusion of all except essential traffic, thus removing the appalling noise, fumes and menace of the heavy traffic which had hitherto streamed through the town centre. Elsewhere the flow of traffic was

167

eased by a one-way street system and by the Inner Distribution Road, the first section of which was opened in 1969. The I.D.R., planned to encircle the town, proved a highly controversial project and met with strong and determined opposition because of the broad path of destruction which was required to make way for it. The road remains unfinished, its second stage ending in mid-air, arrested in its proposed flight across Southampton Street.

Within the finished half of the I.D.R. the western side of the town was transformed by the new Civic Centre complex adjoining the Butts Shopping Centre. The council's decision to build new civic offices was made soon after the war and following on many years of serious overcrowding and inconvenience in the existing municipal buildings put up in the 1870s. The increased size of the borough, from 2,200 acres to 9,100 acres, and the rapidly increasing population, from 32,000 in 1871 to 114,000 in 1951, together with the number of new responsibilities laid upon the council, had caused its departments to overflow into the former abbey hospitium and into an assortment of other offices around the town.

The site chosen for the new Civic Centre was to the west of St Mary's Butts, and the area was gradually cleared of older properties as new housing estates were built further out of town. The new Civic Offices were designed by Robert Matthew, Johnson-Marshall & Partners, and opened in the summer of 1976. The same firm designed the new Thames Valley Police headquarters nearby, and headed the design team for the Hexagon, adjoining the Civic Offices. The Hexagon, one of the most versatile and technologically advanced entertainment centres in the country, was opened in 1977, and filled a long-felt want for a large concert hall and theatre adequately provided with dressing and rehearsal rooms, spacious carpeted foyers with bars, and special facilities for disabled people.

Since the war, changes in regional and local government have removed some of the burdens of responsibility from the borough council. The Local Government Act of 1974 transferred responsibility for major planning matters, roads, social services, education and libraries to Berkshire County Council. The borough had already lost responsibility for its police force, hospitals, fire service and water supply in previous reorganisations which had set up the Thames Valley Police Force, the Regional Hospital Board, the Berkshire and Reading Fire Authority and the Thames Valley Water Board.

In 1977 a small extension of the boundary brought within the borough certain residential areas of Caversham which had grown up

The Hexagon, with the new Civic Centre in the background, from the Inner Distribution Road.

outside it and which belonged rather inconveniently to Oxfordshire. These included Caversham Park Village, an extensive estate of 1,500 houses and bungalows built in the 1960s.

The post-war period has also seen tremendous changes in Reading's industries. The famous three Bs — beer, bulbs and biscuits — have departed, although beer has not gone very far away, and other industries have moved in.

The news that Huntley & Palmers' would be leaving Reading shocked the town in 1972. "Biscuit production at Huntley and Palmers'

King's Road factory is to end", announced the *Chronicle* on 24 November. "In 1976 the huge ovens, which for over a hundred years have baked for every corner of the world, will be shut down. Reading, which owes a great deal of its prosperity to the biscuit factory, was stunned by the news released last week-end. It came from a 'saddened' Mr Alan Palmer, Chairman of Associated Biscuit Manufacturers Ltd. (of which Huntley and Palmers' is a subsidiary). His 'unpleasant' task was due to the essential need for the firm to remain competitive in the biscuit market."

Huntley & Palmers' had merged with Peek Frean in 1921 to form Associated Biscuit Manufacturers Ltd., and in 1960 they had been joined by W & R Jacob. The reasons given for the closure of the factory were the shortage of labour in Reading (a town with one of the lowest unemployment levels in the country), and the age of the factory buildings, which made them unsuitable for the installation of modern machinery without a costly rebuilding programme. Production was to be transferred to the group's other factories at Aintree, Bermondsey and Huyton, which already employed more people and where the higher level of unemployment made recruitment easier. Thus, ironically, the prosperity which Huntley & Palmers' had helped to create was instrumental in driving the firm out of Reading.

The closure of the King's Road factory was phased over several years and was not completed until 1977. For hundreds of employees who had spent their working lives at the factory, as their fathers had done before them, it seemed like the end of an era. Reading could never be the same again. The old factory buildings were soon demolished, and Associated Biscuit Manufacturers retained only administrative offices and warehouses on the King's Road site.

In 1974, after months of speculation, Suttons' announced that they would be moving to Torquay. Seed sales were booming, but the firm was experiencing difficulty in finding part-time labour in Reading, and a proposed new motorway would cut up its trial seed ground. A planned move to a new ground at Twyford had fallen through. Suttons' premises in Market Place were closed in 1974 and the firm severed its connections with the town of its birth in 1976.

In 1960 Simonds' Brewery, by then 175 years old, was taken over by the Courage & Barclay combine and the firm became known as Courage Ltd. Brewing was destined to continue on the historic Bridge Street site for another 20 years, but in 1973 Courage announced its decision to move out of town to a huge 70 acre site at Worton Grange, near the junction of the Basingstoke Road and the M4. The old brewery, with its outdated equipment, limited capacity, and traffic problems in one of the most congested areas of Reading, was to close by the end of the 1970s.

By mid-1977 work on the new brewery was well under way, the nine-acre packaging building and despatch area being due for completion first. In July 1979 all deliveries ceased from Bridge Street, and distribution commenced from the new Berkshire Brewery, using a specially designed fleet of 40 lorries and 80 trailers. Brewing continued at the old brewery until 1980, when that process, too, was transferred. Production at the new brewery, described as the most modern in Europe, is geared to 1,500,000 barrels a year, three times the number previously produced. New methods of brewing have been devised, using stainless steel vessels for the fermenting process and banks of computers to control the various stages of manufacture. The computers themselves are controlled by skilled brewers, whose job it is to ensure that colour, flavour and aroma match up with the highest standards of beer-drinkers in Britain and overseas.

Well before the departure of its older industries Reading had absorbed a number of new industries. Electronic components, data processing, computer software, packaging and containers, pumping equipment, design and engineering services to oil refineries and petrochemical installations, audio and video recording equipment, oils, cables, surgical instruments, joinery products, metal windows and miniature electric motors are the business of just some of today's local firms. Industrial estates have been developed along Basingstoke Road and between the town and the River Thames.

The choice of Reading as the home town of the administrative offices of major concerns moving out of London has brought about dramatic changes in Reading's skyline. Multi-storey buildings have arisen in a variety of shapes and styles. Reading Bridge House, the offices of ICL Dataskil and the first of the giants, was built in 1962-3. Ten years later it was almost dwarfed by the 190 foot Nugent House, offices of the Thames Conservancy. British Rail's 16 storey Western Tower and the looming mass of Foster Wheeler both look down upon the Victorian railway station. Other prominent new buildings which have become familiar parts of the Reading scene are the multi-storey car parks at Yield Hall and Chatham Street, and Forbury House, belonging to the Prudential Assurance Company. Perhaps the most distinguished, however, is Queen's House, opened in 1975, as the prestige headquarters of Metal Box. It has become as well-known a landmark to travellers approaching Reading by rail as Huntley &

Palmers' factory used to be. Its architects were Llewelyn-Davies, Weeks, Forestier-Walker, and Bor.

But for its accessibility by road and river Reading would never have been founded, and if new lines of communication had not passed through it, the town could not have continued to grow. Whenever a speedier means of transport has become available Reading has been well-placed to benefit from it and ready to exploit it. The early people who plodded on foot or horseback along the rough trackways and across the Kennet fords were succeeded centuries later by the dashing vehicles of the coaching age, negotiating the sharp corners in the Bath Road as it passed through Reading. The Regency merchants who fumed at the time it took for their goods to travel along the Kennet & Avon Canal were made happy only decades later by the opening of the Great Western Railway. Little more than a century later their descendants, driving along the A4, may well have sat fuming in their cars as the traffic crawled through the notorious bottleneck at Reading. For these travellers the opening of the M4 on 22 December 1971 was a long-awaited boon. Journey times between London and the west, and between Reading and London were dramatically speeded up.

Queen's House, the headquarters of Metal Box, Ltd.

Reading was relieved of much of the burden of traffic which had passed through it and was conveniently linked via three interchanges with the motorway as it passed to the south of the town. Five years later an even speedier journey was offered by British Rail, whose Inter City 125 trains could travel the 112 miles between Paddington and Bristol in 73 minutes. History was made on 30 September 1976 when the first 125 train hurtled through Reading on a trial run from Paddington to Cardiff. A week later the new trains entered regular service on the Western Region main line, and for Reading commuters it meant that London was a mere 23 minutes away.

The increasing proximity to London and the changes to social and business patterns which accompanied it, contributed to the problem faced by the town in the 1950s and 1960s. Was it losing its identity? Was it still a place that people could be proud to call their home town? Reading in recent years has been called Britain's Average Town, The Town for a Full Life, The Total Town, A Town of Today, and, less favourably, 'a cold cancer of a town', Dragsville, 'a dull town, too near London to have any life of its own'. The charge of dullness is not new to Reading. More than a century ago the *Berkshire Chronicle*, commenting on what was thought to be the end of cheap rail fares, remarked that "these monstrous facilities of travelling" had taught Reading people to regard their town merely as a place to get money in, and London as the centre of enjoyment in which to spend it. "Reading shops, Reading pleasures and Reading faces must be our common sight and daily food", the writer declared.

But it was true that Reading, at that time (1858), had little to offer in the way of recreation. Its single theatre was moribund; there were occasional concerts and lectures in the Town Hall and in the New Hall in London Street; there was a commercial lending library; but there was no public library, museum or art gallery, and there were no public parks or playing fields.

The latter part of the 19th century was to change all that. Increasing commercial prosperity, the enterprise and philanthropy of the town's leading citizens, and renewed activity on the part of the borough council brought about tremendous improvments in the town's amenities; and, as the 20th century progressed, two flourishing commercial theatres and nearly a dozen cinemas provided a wide choice of entertainment.

In the late 1950s, following on the long years of austerity, dullness began to take over again. The cinemas had helped to kill off the theatres and now television had killed off half the cinemas. There was,

Reading Station, whose present central building was opened in 1869, with Nugent House and Reading Bridge House in the background.

besides, an acute shortage of public halls with facilities for putting on amateur concerts or dramatic productions. The Town Hall, opened in 1882 and sadly lacking in dressing rooms or other provisions for performers, was the only hall large enough to accommodate professional concerts or performances by the major local musical societies, such as the Sainsbury Singers, Reading Festival Chorus, Reading Symphony Orchestra, the Arion Orchestra and Moods in Music. Several smaller societies, such as Reading Amateur Operatic Society, the Earley Players and St Laurence Players, helped to keep entertainment live by performing in various uncomfortable and inadequate halls around the town. The enterprising and very successful Progress Theatre Group founded their own theatre in a hut off Christchurch road in 1951 and gradually raised enough money to transform it into one of the best small theatres in the country, with standards high enough to win it membership of the Little Theatre Guild of Great Britain.

Nevertheless, in spite of all these efforts and the efforts of the many other local societies, Reading's reputation was falling. In 1968 the

174

residents of the new Caversham Park Village housing estate forcibly expressed their opinion. "Reading", they said, "must be the deadest, dullest, most boring dragsville with the powers and dignity of a County Borough."

"Reading is Dragsville", shouted the *Chronicle* provocatively across its front page on 15 March 1968, and further comments made by the Caversham Park Village Association were reported. "Reading is a No Town", "Reading is dead", "There is no professional theatre, no concert hall, and the Town Hall is so gloomy", "It is a drag for the children." The Mayor, Alderman Francis Taylor, indignantly denied the charges, and although some people sympathised with the Caversham Park residents, many more thought that Reading was not as bad as all that.

A year later the Borough Council and the Reading Chamber of Commerce and Trade began to discuss plans for a gigantic Reading Festival to be held in the summer of 1971. A month-long programme of events was to be designed to show that Reading was a Total Town, embracing every aspect of living, and able to boast of its achievements in industry, trade, commerce, sport, entertainment, culture and education. The Festival would at the same time celebrate the 1100th anniversary of the town's first mention in recorded history in 871, and the 800th anniversary of the foundation of Reading Abbey in 1121. There was to be a shopping festival involving all the local shops, and a great Reading Industries Exhibition, which it was hoped would attract businessmen from around the world. The Reading Festival was to be the biggest event of its kind in the south of England in 1971.

Unfortunately, three months before the Festival was due to start, the Industries Exhibition had to be cancelled. A winter of industrial unrest followed by a long postal strike and the consequent shortage of time for preparation made it impossible for enough firms to take part. A blow to the Shopping Festival was a delay in the completion of the Butts Centre, the opening of which had been planned as a major event. Nevertheless the Festival went ahead with a full and varied programme of events organised by local societies, firms, churches, schools, the University, British Rail and the borough council departments. The numerous events included a carnival procession, a beer festival, a performance of *Macbeth* by the Berkshire Shakespeare Players in the abbey ruins, Reading Regatta and other water sports, football and cricket matches, concerts, flower shows, a rabbit show, a Victorian Weekend organised by the parishioners of All Saints' Church, poetry readings, art exhibitions, open days, lectures, dances and a display of mediaeval jousting in Prospect Park. The Festival enjoyed a very considerable local success, but it did not, as had been hoped, have much impact further afield.

If Reading did not quite prove itself The Total Town it has, in recent years, gained a reputation as Britain's Average Town. Its medium size between a small town and a city, its busy and prosperous shopping centre containing a range of shops representative of those to be found in towns all over Britain, its shopping population drawn from a wide area and a wide variety of occupations, as well as its accessibility, have made it a mecca for market research workers and an ideal place for trying out new products.

The national reality of being Britain's Average Town came one morning in April 1974. On the previous evening the first part had been shown on television of a BBC documentary intended to show the everyday life of an ordinary British family. The Wilkins family, whose nine members, a cat and several cages of budgerigars lived in a six-roomed flat in Reading, had been selected out of hundreds of candidates. The highly unconventional domestic set-up revealed upon the screen, the frank, unscripted conversations and arguments, the forthright opinions of Mrs Wilkins, shocked the nation's viewers.

"Disgusting", screamed hundreds of letters and several newspapers. "It's insulting to Reading", protested local residents. "This town used to be known for its A4 traffic jams. Now it's known for where the terrible Wilkins live." The *Sunday Times,* however, pronouned the programme "the most radical experiment in public access to television we have so far had. . . vastly entertaining." The *Guardian* said, "It is a glorious programme and not without honour, save in its own city."

Reading took the ballyhoo in its stride. It had, after all, learned to live, since 1971, with an open-air Rock Festival, held at August Bank Holiday weekends on a 55 acre site between the Thames and Richfield Avenue. By 1975 the event, organised by the National Jazz Federation, had become so popular that an estimated 50,000 fans streamed into Reading and converged upon a site designed to hold 30,000. Local residents, who had complained in previous years, got together and petitioned the council to ban the festival in future. Complaints were made about the noise, the dirt, the litter, the breaking down of fences to light fires, the looting of vegetables from the adjoining allotments, obscenities broadcast over the public address system and nude exhibitionists on the Thames Side Promenade. The council was divided on the issue, Conservative members being anxious to move the festival from the Richfield Avenue site and Labour members willing to let it stay. The festival continues.

Since The Hexagon was opened in 1977 a whole new range of professional entertainment has been brought to the town, and indeed to the whole Thames Valley region. First class orchestras, soloists, actors and comedians can now be tempted to appear in Reading, and often play to packed houses. The Hexagon is also used for performances by the leading local orchestras and operatic societies. Good entertainment has greatly improved the quality of life in Reading.

The town can boast over 500 local societies, enabling people to pursue an astonishingly wide variety of leisure interests and activities. Among the larger societies is the Reading Horticultural Federation which, for 40 years, has organised the annual Reading Show, one of the biggest of its kind in the south of England and a popular shop window for the activities and achievements of other local societies.

Reading Amateur Regatta is held every summer on the Thames above Caversham Bridge. The Reading University Head of the River Race held each March for the last 40 years is the first major event in the British Rowing Calendar. Reading Swimming Club meets at the large modern Central Swimming Pool, where facilities include instruction in swimming and life saving. The Club holds frequent galas. Professional soccer can be seen at Elm Park, where Reading F.C. play in the Football League.

Reading Camera Club and the Reading Guild of Artists put on annual exhibitions in Reading Art Gallery. Reading Civic Society and Reading Waterways Trust endeavour to preserve and encourage interest in the town's historic remains and amenities. The Reading branch of the Kennet & Avon Canal Trust has helped in the arduous task of restoring the canal for leisure use. The Reading Centre of the National Trust is one of the largest and most active in the country, and arranges lectures by eminent speakers and visits to historic houses. Berkshire's first National Trust house, Basildon Park, was opened to the public in 1979. Reading University welcomes townspeople to its Film Theatre in Whiteknights Park.

Something of Reading's history can be seen at Reading Museum, where, in addition to the famous collection of Roman remains from Silchester, fresh exhibitions are regularly arranged to show other fascinating material from the Museum's vast collections.

Reading is the home of one of the newest newspapers in Britain.

When the *Evening Post* was started on 14 September 1965 it was not only the country's first new paper since before the second world war but the first newspaper in the world to be produced by using together the three techniques of computer setting, photo-composition and web offset.

Its founder was Canadian businessman Roy Thomson, then head of the Thomson Organisation in Britain, which owned, among other concerns, the mighty *Times*. The *Evening Post* grew out of the *Reading Standard,* a lively and popular weekly which had been published in Reading since 1891. The *Evening Post* now employs 400 people and is printed at its head office and works in Tessa Road on the Richfield Avenue industrial estate. Visitors from newspapers all over the world have come to study its modern, and constantly updated, production methods. The paper now has a daily sale of 50,000 and circulates as far afield as Newbury, Basingstoke, Bracknell, Wokingham, Maidenhead, Henley and Wallingford.

Another new media enterprise is Reading's local commercial radio station, Radio 210, which first went on the air on 8 march 1976. From its base in Calcot Radio 210 broadcasts 19 hours a day, from 6 a.m. until 1 a.m. the following morning. Its programmes are a mixture of music and news, ranging from the very local to international coverage. It is a community-conscious station, and as well as providing essential local information it is willing to help charitable causes.

Reading Bridge in the 1950s.

Reading's reputation has changed over the centuries along with its changing fortunes, and the many names and opinions which it has inspired, or sometimes provoked, reflect the town's adaptability and capacity to survive as well as its strengths and weaknesses.

In early mediaeval times its abbey made it a great centre of pilgrimage; in later mediaeval times it was, as John Leland said, a town which chiefly stood by its clothing trade. In the 19th century it became famous as The Biscuit Town, or, as one laudatory poem put it, The Biscuit City. Thomas Hardy, in his Wessex novels, called it, just as appropriately, Aldbrickham. Britain's Average Town, A Town of Today, The Town for a Full Life; call it what you will. Certainly it would now be a churlish person who called the town a dull one. Greater Reading, now home for nearly 200,000 people has a vitality which shows no signs of diminishing.

A List of Principal Sources and Suggestions for Further Reading

Anderson, A.H.   Reading and its surroundings. 1906.

Anglo-Saxon chronicle; edited by B. Thorpe. 1861.

Appleby, H.M.   The Kendrick book. 1948.

Arnold, H.G.   Victorian architecture in Reading. 1976.

Braithwaite, W.C.   Lessons from early Quakerism in Reading. 1913.

Burton, K.G.   The early newspaper press in Berkshire. 1954.

Burton, K.G.   A reception town in war and peace: some aspects of life in Reading, 1938-50. 1955.

Childs, W.M.   Making a university. 1933.

Childs, W.M.   The town of Reading during the early part of the 19th century. 1910.

Clark, M.   The cloth trade of Reading. (unpublished MS. n.d.)

Clew, K.   The Kennet and Avon canal. 1973.

Coates, C.   The history and antiquities of Reading. 1802.

Corley, T.A.B.   Quaker enterprise in biscuits: Huntley and Palmers of Reading 1822-1972. 1972.

Darby, H.C. and Campbell, E.M.J.   The Domesday geography of south-east England. 1962.

Darter, W.S.   Reminiscences of Reading. 1888.

Darton, F.J.   The life and times of Mrs Sherwood. 1910.

Disbury, D.G.   Berkshire in the Civil War. 1978.

Dormer, E.W.   The parish and church of St Peter, Earley. 1944.

Gillett, H.M.   The restored shine of Our Lady of Caversham. 1958.

Guilding, J.M.   Reading records: the diary of the Corporation, 1431-1654. 1892-6. 4 vols.

Harman, L.   The history of christianity in Reading. 1952.

Harman, L.   The parish of S. Giles-in-Reading. 1946.

Hinton, M.   A history of the town of Reading. 1954.

Holzman, J.M.   The Nabobs in England. 1926.

Humphreys, A.L.   Caversham Bridge 1231-1926. 1926.

Hurry, J.B.   Reading Abbey. 1901.

Jordan, H.E.   The tramways of Reading. 1957.

Kemp, B.R.   Reading Abbey. 1968.

Lee, W.   Report to the General Board of Health. 1850.

Luke, S.   Journal, 1643-4; edited by I.G. Philip, 1949-53. 3 vols.

Man, J. The stranger in Reading. 1810.

Paul, J.E.   The last abbot of Reading. 1961.

Preston, A.E.   The demolition of Reading Abbey. 1935.

Pritchard, C.F.   Reading charters, acts and orders, 1253-1911. 1913.

Reading War Hospitals Supplies Depot. Friends of the wounded.
    c. 1919.

Ridgway, J.   A brief account of Caversham. 1861.

Slade, C.F.   Reading. 1969. (Historic Towns series)

Smith, E.   A history of Whiteknights. 1957.

Spriggs, F.G.   History of the church of Greyfriars, Reading. 1963.

Stenton, F.M.   Anglo-Saxon England. 1971.

Sutton's at Reading. 1923.

Victoria History of Berkshire. 1906-27. 4 vols.

Watts, J.   A Black scene opened; being the true state of Mr John
    Kendrick's gifts to the town of Reading. 1749.

Watts, J.   Memorandums of John Watts, Esq. Mayor of Reading
    1722-23 and 1728-9; edited by K.G. Burton. 1950.

All these books are in the Local History Collection at Reading Library.
Many of the more recent publications are available for loan.

Index